# Service Science and the Information Professional

## CHANDOS
### INFORMATION PROFESSIONAL SERIES
Series Editor: Ruth Rikowski
(email: Rikowskigr@aol.com)

Chandos' new series of books is aimed at the busy information professional. They have been specially commissioned to provide the reader with an authoritative view of current thinking. They are designed to provide easy-to-read and (most importantly) practical coverage of topics that are of interest to librarians and other information professionals. If you would like a full listing of current and forthcoming titles, please visit www.chandospublishing.com.

**New authors:** we are always pleased to receive ideas for new titles; if you would like to write a book for Chandos, please contact Dr. Glyn Jones at g.jones.2@elsevier.com or by telephone +44 (0) 1865 843000.

# Service Science and the Information Professional

YVONNE DE GRANDBOIS

AMSTERDAM • BOSTON • HEIDELBERG • LONDON
NEW YORK • OXFORD • PARIS • SAN DIEGO
SAN FRANCISCO • SINGAPORE • SYDNEY • TOKYO
Chandos Publishing is an imprint of Elsevier

Chandos Publishing is an imprint of Elsevier
225 Wyman Street, Waltham, MA 02451, USA
Langford Lane, Kidlington, OX5 1GB, UK

Copyright © 2016 by Y. de Grandbois. Published by Elsevier Ltd. All rights reserved.

No part of this publication may be reproduced or transmitted in any form or by any means, electronic or mechanical, including photocopying, recording, or any information storage and retrieval system, without permission in writing from the publisher. Details on how to seek permission, further information about the Publisher's permissions policies and our arrangements with organizations such as the Copyright Clearance Center and the Copyright Licensing Agency, can be found at our website: www.elsevier.com/permissions.

This book and the individual contributions contained in it are protected under copyright by the Publisher (other than as may be noted herein).

**Notices**
Knowledge and best practice in this field are constantly changing. As new research and experience broaden our understanding, changes in research methods, professional practices, or medical treatment may become necessary.

Practitioners and researchers must always rely on their own experience and knowledge in evaluating and using any information, methods, compounds, or experiments described herein. In using such information or methods they should be mindful of their own safety and the safety of others, including parties for whom they have a professional responsibility.

To the fullest extent of the law, neither the Publisher nor the authors, contributors, or editors, assume any liability for any injury and/or damage to persons or property as a matter of products liability, negligence or otherwise, or from any use or operation of any methods, products, instructions, or ideas contained in the material herein.

ISBN: 978-1-84334-649-4

**British Library Cataloguing-in-Publication Data**
A catalogue record for this book is available from the British Library.

Library of Congress Control Number: 2015944393

For Information on all Chandos Publishing publications
visit our website at http://store.elsevier.com/

Transferred to Digital Printing, 2015

# DEDICATION

To Julien, Julia, and Johan.

# CONTENTS

*Readers Info* — xi
*Acknowledgements* — xiii
*Prologue* — xv

**1. Service, Systems, and Science** — 1

A Service is... — 1
Service Defined — 2
Service Described: The IHIP Paradigm — 3
Classifying Services — 4
The Standard Industrial Classification — 5
Typologies of Services — 6
Trade of Goods and Services — 6
Products and Services and Their Differences — 7
The Product-Service Continuum — 7
Organizational Models — 8
Risk Factors — 9
The Contact Factor — 10
Service-Dominant view — 10
Self-Service — 12
Self-Service Technologies — 12
Super Service — 13
Sustainability and Services — 14
What Is a Service System? — 14
Systems and Functions — 15
Holistic Service Systems — 17
Service Systems Expand — 17
Service Systems in Information Work — 18
Library 2.0 and the Long Tail — 20
How to Apply the Long Tail to Information Work — 21
Library 3.0 — 22
The Knowledge Economy and Life-Long Learning — 22
The International Information Sector — 23
Research4Life — 24
The Bigger Picture — 24
References — 25

## 2. The Story of Service Science — 27

| | |
|---|---|
| The Shift to a Knowledge Economy | 27 |
| Agricultural, Industrial, and Post-Industrial Economies | 27 |
| Types of Economic Sectors | 28 |
| The Economic Importance of Services | 29 |
| The Servitization of Business | 30 |
| The Rise of the Service Sector | 31 |
| Reasons for the Shift | 31 |
| In Tandem with the Shift? | 33 |
| Toward an Economy of Service and Knowledge | 34 |
| The IBM Story | 37 |
| Getting Started | 39 |
| Service Science | 40 |
| Basic Components | 41 |
| Who Can Benefit from Service Science? | 43 |
| Forward into Satisfaction | 44 |
| References | 46 |

## 3. Synergies: Service Science and the Information Sector — 47

| | |
|---|---|
| Participating in the Service Science Explosion | 47 |
| Information Professionals and Service | 47 |
| The Economy and Service Science | 48 |
| The Energy of New Vistas | 49 |
| Research Opportunities | 49 |
| Two Major Studies for Research Priorities in Services | 50 |
| Fast Forward to 2015 | 58 |
| A New Profile for the Knowledge Worker | 59 |
| An Academic Home for Service Science | 62 |
| iSchools | 62 |
| The iSchool Proposal | 64 |
| Who is Teaching What? | 66 |
| What are iSchools Teaching? | 70 |
| An Outside Opinion | 72 |
| A Service Science Look at Libraries | 72 |
| Moving On | 73 |
| References | 73 |

## 4. Service Science for a Smarter Planet — 75

| | |
|---|---|
| A Smarter Planet | 75 |
| The Internet of Things | 77 |
| IoT Comes on Stage | 78 |

|  |  |
|---|---|
| Other Practical Applications | 79 |
| Early Thought Leaders | 80 |
| Big Data | 81 |
| Not Only Big Business | 82 |
| Analytics | 84 |
| Cloud Computing | 85 |
| Cognitive Computing | 86 |
| The Circular Economy | 87 |
| Smarter Planet Initiative | 87 |
| Another Opinion | 89 |
| Smarter Cities | 89 |
| Other Concepts of Whole Service Cities | 92 |
| Making a Difference | 93 |
| Service Science and Social Value | 93 |
| Instrumented, Interconnected, Intelligent | 94 |
| References | 96 |

## 5. Credit, Community, and Questions — 99

|  |  |
|---|---|
| The Ground Work: Giving Credit | 99 |
| The Community | 101 |
| Some Questions | 104 |
| References | 107 |

*Epilogue* — *109*
*Index* — *113*

# READERS INFO

Readers: In the e-version of the book, you are requested to refer to the hyperlinked terms and websites with the running text (of each chapter), which will in-turn direct you to the WebCite-enhanced reference which contains—in addition to the original live URL—a link to an archived copy of the material, exactly as it was when last accessed. This will enable you to have permanent access to the cited material avoiding cases of the site becoming inactive or content changes expected over a period of time.

# ACKNOWLEDGEMENTS

I am grateful to my colleagues and friends at the University of Western Switzerland, Geneva, where I began to study Service Science and then was caught up in the energy surrounding it. And I am grateful to the Montreux Business University for their encouragement of this project.

I have never met Jim Spohrer in person, but I know him through his work and his writings. Thank you, Jim, for your energy and passion not only for Service Science, but for everything you so ably keep up with on the leading edge and then tell us about in such an interesting way.

Many, many thanks to Paul Maglio, for all you have contributed to and written about Service Science. The dynamic way in which you teach this subject is an inspiration to me. Your immediate and generous response to my request to use your syllabus in the book and for my teaching was a model of service! Your help is gratefully acknowledged.

Thank you to Corrado Pettenati, former Head of the Scientific Information Service of the CERN (European Organization for Nuclear Research), who read the very first draft. Corrado is a scientist, a techie, and an information specialist and I knew he would give straight feedback. He did, and his enthusiastic endorsement was key in continuing the project.

Thank you to Linda Stoddart, former Academic Director of the Master of Science in Information and Knowledge Strategy, Columbia University, who put the finger on what I was doing when I could go no further. She told me I was bringing in new knowledge, describing new paths. Linda gave me her copy of Prusak's *Working Knowledge*, and said— "he did it for knowledge management, you're doing it for Service Science." Something clicked. I finished the book.

Much appreciation for their expertise, patience, and encouragement goes to George Knott, my Editor; Harriet Clayton, Managing Editor; Omer Mukthar Moosa, Project Manager; and Hop Wechsler, Permissions Help desk Manager; all from Elsevier. You are a great team, and Elsevier's authors are extremely fortunate to be able to work with you.

To all the amazing information professionals I have had the good fortune to know—with a special mention to the LINK team at the World Health Organization.

To my family, source of everything good, thank you.

# PROLOGUE

I was having lunch with one of the top professors in the management faculty of a University in Switzerland. I was new at the school, and excited about being able to share my experience with these young people who had chosen the information profession. On the walk from the school to the restaurant, the professor said something that was obvious to him but shocking to me. He said that in his opinion the information professions would go the way of the mail carrier and the travel agent—they would soon be obsolete. He maintained that, too often, these professions gave people services they thought they should have, and this was usually a one-size fits all. However, the market was not responding to this. He was very clear in his thought—giving me a readout that I found was fairly common in his department. My own experience had me on a totally different wavelength. I had never paid attention to those negative articles that would appear in the professional literature. The people I knew in the information professions were smart, passionate, and committed and did not have the time to ruminate about their profile. They mostly thought they had the best jobs in the world and were enjoying a career where you got paid for learning, growing, meeting interesting people, and staying on the leading edge of knowledge and technology.

On the first day of classes at the post graduate School of Information Studies I attended we were told by the director that upon graduating from this school the world would be our oyster. The phrase seemed absurd at the time. In retrospect however, it proved itself true, opening so many doors in so many disciplines. I especially remember a professor that inflamed and inspired us with her passion for knowledge and the profession we would be entering. She would have us stand up and express ourselves over and over until we learned to hold the audience in the palm of our hands and stream our message with ease. We were simply not allowed to be silent or timid, and this was taught in such an engaging and humorous way that we would have followed her anywhere.

My career path led to working in just about every sector of the information realm on two continents: public, private, academic, government, regional, school, and three mandates in the international sector. Oyster indeed! My longest international mandate was as Coordinator of the World Health Organization's Library and Information Networks for

Knowledge (LINK). After that I began teaching at the bachelor and master levels and was responsible for a new master's program in the Information Studies Department between two universities in Canada and Switzerland. In coming to this university, I knew what I wanted to transmit. I was armed with a thousand examples of real life experience, most of which had been rich and stimulating and rewarding (especially in retrospect!).

It was at this university, in a faculty other than mine, where I discovered Service Science.

At the start of this move to academia, I was invited to give a class at the university. The audience included the Dean, the head of the Department of Information Studies, the head of the Research Department, and two professors. The topic I was given was *Service Science and Its Relationship to Information Science.*

At the time, I had not yet made a connection between Service Science and Information Science. I thought surely there would be something written on this in the professional literature (this was 2009). Wrong. Although there were articles about Service Science, very little was related to the information professions. I spoke to many brilliant and capable knowledge workers in the international sector, and they actually had never heard of Service Science, but, like me, wanted to know more about it. So I plunged into it and the more I studied Service Science, the more I learned not only about its relationship to Information Science, but its absolute relevance to our entire profession, and its place in the world.

Although a young discipline, Service Science has many proponents, some in prestigious universities, and others in the private sector. As I researched the topic, I became convinced that this was a theme that information professionals needed to know about and to be involved in. If any profession today was dealing with people, technology, organizations and information, it was the knowledge worker in information. The growing number of universities that taught Service Science taught it through faculties not related to Information Science, with a few exceptions such as the iSchools at the University of California at Berkeley and the University of Toronto.

I began by using my bachelor-, and then master-level students as a forum to test the water on this topic. I gave classes on Service Science in my marketing and client relationship management courses and invited guest speakers to explore and expand this concept. The students responded positively to the classes. They considered it totally normal that they study Service Science. We had many fine discussions as to the place of Service Science in the information economy and in their future work. We looked at the importance of linking research and "real life," and staying ahead of the game: interacting with and learning about different disciplines and professions, embracing change and innovation, moving forward.

I presented a paper on Service Science at an Online Information conference in London. This important annual conference is aimed at information professionals, analysts, and researchers in all sectors; IT professionals; publishers; and senior executives responsible for information strategy. The paper was selected to be part of the theme, "Broadening our horizons: fresh insights and opportunities to stay ahead." I write this book in this spirit by sharing a subject that I think is important and necessary to our future.

When I began researching this fascinating story and writing this book, I looked at Service Science from the point of view of a practitioner and professor of information. The sectors I wanted to reach included information professionals, students and professors in schools of information, and iSchools. Service Science is something we as information professionals should know and incorporate in our minds, our work, our research, and our curricula. We give service within service systems, and deal with people, technology, organization, and information. We are T-shaped professionals in that we have advanced degrees in specialized areas, with a wide horizontal background including information, technology, communication, and the social sciences. We are curious to know about other disciplines in order to do a good job. We are team players. All of this leads to a natural connection to Service Science.

As I kept researching and writing about Service Science, I found that this material is also relevant and timely for management and business schools, IT specialists, service industries, companies interested in the economic value of information, and the curious individual wanting to discover something new. My Swiss banker friends want to know all about it! One thing is certain—this question always comes up: "Service Science? What's that?!" People genuinely want to know.

Many of the articles on Service Science are found in technical, specialized literature, and I have kept the explanations as clear as possible, distilled from the reams of material I studied. You may simply be interested in learning something new, or you may want to investigate the topic further. This book will give you the basics, and point the way to further study.

Here you will find a general overview of service, service systems, and Service Science as it pertains to the information economy and the information professions. This new discipline is very close to our goals and our work, and contributes to our professional development and interest. Service Science is not necessarily something we would have studied in our post-graduate education, as it is still emerging. There is little written on the topic in our theoretical, practical, and research literature. The articles on Service Science in the engineering, technical, management, and business arenas do not necessarily come across our desk every day. This book is intended to inform you on the subject in an easy and interesting way.

First we will briefly discuss service and its attributes. Then we will look at service systems and how they operate. This leads to an introduction to the new discipline of Service Science and the fascinating story of how it began. We will consider the relationship between Service Science and Information Science, why it is important to us, why we are important to it, and how it redefines the profile of the knowledge worker. Finally, we will look at options and ideas as to how to incorporate Service Science into our existing body of knowledge, citing some examples that are already taking shape. We will describe some of the future directions that Service Science is defining on a world scale. We will see who the players in this field are, and what they are saying.

This fascinating new frontier that is determinedly making its mark in the knowledge economy continues to be a learning process for me, even beyond the completion of this book. The momentum of its growth and development is extremely rapid, and it just keeps coming. I hope that it will spark new thoughts and ideas for you, no matter what your background.

In today's wonderful, connected world, we are all information specialists. And we are all knowledge workers. We prefer to stay on the leading edge, where ideas are new, and where there is room to grow.

Enjoy reading this book—it is not often that we find ourselves at the very start of a subject or movement that will have great impact in the time to come.

# CHAPTER 1

# Service, Systems, and Science

*I slept and I dreamed that life is all joy. I woke and I saw that life is all service. I served and I saw that service is joy.*

*Rabindranath Tagore*

## A SERVICE IS...

We use, receive or give services every single day without giving it a thought. For example, we greet the mail carrier who puts the mail in our mailbox, we go to the hairdresser to cut our hair, we get the car washed on the way home, and we pay the student who walked the dog while we were gone. We call our IT professional to set up our new computer, we have lunch with a friend at the new Italian restaurant, we go the bank, we buy a nice dessert to accompany dinner, and we decide on a film for the evening after our Yoga class. All of these interactions involve a service.

Services exist on a larger scale as well. Local governments provide public services such as police protection, firefighting, roads, electricity, gas, water, phone lines, garbage removal, and a multitude of other infrastructures, and provide for their maintenance and repair. Transportation systems provide the services of public utility vehicles, such as buses, trains, ships, ferries and airlines. The people who do this work offer a tremendous array of services that make our lives one of safety, comfort, and ease.

Healthcare and medical services are given in hospitals, clinics and specialized care homes.

Education is a major service industry and takes a 10% share of the GDP in the United States. Some would consider it one of the most important service sectors, and a basic need of society. Public and private schools offer educational services from preschool through university, and specialized post-graduate institutions provide a platform for learning, growth, and advancement opportunities.

The information, communications, and technology sectors provide us with phones, computers, the Internet, television, radio, newspapers, magazines, and other media.

*Service Science and the Information Professional.*
© 2016 by Y. de Grandbois. Published by Elsevier Ltd. All rights reserved.

Professional services are rendered by our doctor, lawyer, accountant, architect, librarian, teacher, engineer, consultant, musician, computer programmer, reporter, and so on. Service jobs include those of a waiter, receptionist, sales clerk, IT help desk, plumber, electrician, carpenter, mason, repairman, office assistant, cashier, translator, tour guide, caterer, cook, window cleaner, beauty salon operator—the list is long.

Then there are the retail and wholesale services that sell us their wares in shopping malls, department stores, boutiques, grocery stores, and online. Real estate agents give us the services that allow us to buy, rent, and sell property. And food services offered by restaurants, cafeterias, fast food chains, and stores give us pleasure and satisfaction in our work or leisure time.

Business services such as professional services, financial services, and transportation exist to facilitate other businesses.

There are a myriad of hospitality and leisure services such as travel services, hotels, restaurants, spas, ski resorts, sports clubs, fitness centers, museums, parks, campgrounds, and cinemas. Leisure and recreational services have grown into a multibillion dollar business worldwide as people have more time and more means to enjoy time that is not spent at work.

And not to forget Nature, and the gifts that she provides, read this little verse, *To a Child, Written in Her Album*, by William Wordsworth:

> "Small service is true service while it lasts:
> Of humblest friends, bright Creature! scorn not one;
> The Daisy, by the shadow that it casts,
> Protects the lingering dew drop from the Sun."

## SERVICE DEFINED

There has been a revision of the standard definition of service in the last 20 years because different disciplines have given their own definitions, including economics, marketing, operations, industrial and systems engineering, and computer science.

Here are a few examples of definitions of service in the literature over the years:

- *Activities, benefits, and satisfactions which are offered for sale or are provided in connection with the sale of goods* (The American Marketing Association, 1960).
- *A service is a change in the condition of a person, or a good belonging to some economic entity, brought about as the result of the activity of some other economic entity, with the approval of the first person or economic entity* (Hill, 1977).

- *All economic activity whose output is not a physical product or construction* (Baruch, Quinn, & Cushman Paquette, 1987).
- *An activity or series of activities . . . provided as solution to customer problems* (Gronroos, 1990).
- *Deeds, processes, performances* (Zeithaml & Bitner, 1996).
- *Application of competences for the benefit of another entity* (Vargo & Lusch, 2004).
- *A time-perishable, intangible experience performed for a customer acting in the role of co-producer* (Fitzsimmons & Fitzsimmons, 2005).

Simply put, services are the application of knowledge for mutual benefit between entities. This appears to be the definition today. In all cases, service involves the deployment of knowledge, skills, and competencies that one person or organization does for the benefit of another.

## SERVICE DESCRIBED: THE IHIP PARADIGM

Going further, a service can be described (rather than defined) by several main attributes. The IHIP paradigm (Lovelock & Gummesson, 2004) is normally used to describe service activities.

For example, a service is *intangible*—it is a transaction rather than a physical product. You can't see it or hold it or smell it. Services are ideas and concepts that are part of a process and the client typically relies on the service provider's reputation, knowledge, and skills to help predict quality and to make service choices. A physician who visits a patient and prescribes a remedy provides an intangible service. A motivational speaker who delivers a powerful speech to inspire managers is another example of an intangible service.

Because service is based on a process of co-creation between the provider and the client, it is *heterogeneous* because the interactions between the provider and client are unique and different each time. Personalization of services increases their heterogeneous nature, since the service is modified for each client or each situation; for example, a medical consultation, a haircut, or a visit to our accountant, tax assessor, or ski instructor. No consultation with one of these services would ever be identical to the one before. Each visit would be unique, even if the service provider and the client are the same.

A service also has the attribute of *inseparability*: the service provider and the service consumer must be involved in the transaction. For example, the service consumer must be in the restaurant as well as the cook and waiter in order for a transaction to take place. The accountant calculates a tax return with the information given to him or her by the client. The plumber comes to the house to repair something at the request of the owner. Quality control can be achieved only after consumption.

Finally, service benefits are created and consumed at the same time, as in the example of medical care, and therefore they are considered *perishable*. Services cannot be inventoried or stored and used another time. Therefore, any service capacity that goes unused is lost, and thus it is also a lost economic opportunity as well.

Two more attributes to the IHIP paradigm were later added, those of client-based relationships and customer contact.

There has been a lively debate in the literature concerning the validity of the IHIP paradigm. It is not our intention to go into that discussion, but it is useful to know that it is taking place. A clear summary of this debate can be found in the chapter by Sampson in the *Handbook of Service Science* (Maglio, Kieliszewski, & Spohrer, 2010). Sampson presents a case for using the Unified Service Theory (UST) paradigm instead. The UST takes into account input components, customers, and production processes. The main difference is that customer inputs are the defining features of service as long as the customer is identified and the process being analyzed is specified. It comes from a process perspective—that is, services are composed of processes that transform inputs into outputs.

A recent study (Ostrom, Parasuraman, Bowen, Patricio, & Voss, 2015) states that the IHIP paradigm was largely dismissed by the service-dominant logic perspective. However, Ostrom's study maintains that there is support in their findings for the theoretical value of both perspectives, that of the IHIP paradigm and service-dominant logic.

## CLASSIFYING SERVICES

In marketing and economics a service is a nonmaterial equivalent of a product or a good. It is an economic activity that does not result in ownership. In national economic statistics, the service sector is often defined as whatever is *not* agriculture or manufacturing. The Economist humorously describes services as products of economic activity that you can't drop on your foot! It then goes on to say,

> *In most countries, the share of economic activity accounted for by services rose steadily during the twentieth century at the expense of agriculture and manufacturing. More than two-thirds of output in OECD countries, and up to four-fifths of employment, is now in the services sector*
>
> ***(Economist; see References)***

## THE STANDARD INDUSTRIAL CLASSIFICATION

Services began to be classified by the United States Department of Commerce Standard Industrial Classification codes established in the 1930s, when services appeared as a residual category. The Standard Industrial Classification (SIC) is a US government system for classifying industries in the principle segments of the economy by a four-digit numerical code. The broad divisions such as agriculture, mining, construction, manufacturing, and such are then broken down according to the major groups within the division, and from there divided according to the products within the major groups. For example, under the division of manufacturing is listed the major group of food and kindred products. Then under this, the products are listed by industry group such as meat products, followed by specific products such as bacon, and so on. In other words, this is a huge classification system that lists what is produced, bought, and sold, and provides a system for quantifying these transactions. Isn't this amazing? These statistics can be used as a reflection of how the economy is operating in the different sectors. Since 1997 the SIC has been replaced by the six-digit North American Industry Classification System (NAICS code), which basically follows the same logic, but includes Canadian and Mexican industries as well.

Services were classed as a residual category when the SIC was established because at that time the main economic sectors were agriculture and manufacturing. Today services are the fastest growing part of economic activity in advanced economies. Services have become a major force and have a larger place in the world economy than manufacturing. This has been further enabled by advancements in technology, telecommunications, and of course the Internet, factors that have allowed the trade of services on an international scale. The Internet especially, as a dynamic platform, makes an exchange of services possible on a worldwide scale, both on an individual and a corporate level. Never before have people in almost any country been able to market their services or products or ideas across borders with such ease.

The SIC example is given to illustrate how a national classification system works. However, each nation has its own, and the United Nations Department of Economic and Social Affairs website (http://www.webcitation.org/6abBdN2us) publishes the national classifications of 154 countries by region: Africa, North America, South America, Asia, Europe, and Oceania. This website includes 448 current classifications.

The general structure of most of these classifications resemble each other, with national specificities added where needed.

## TYPOLOGIES OF SERVICES

Bryson, Daniels, and Warf (2004) provide a typology of services that encompass a list of service values based on core service experience, bringing the classes into an even finer level. The list includes values such as creative, enabling, experiential, information, innovation, problem solving, quality of life, and others. Other typologies have been described, using the term holistic, but most of these are based on the Bryson model (Glückler & Hammer, 2011).

## TRADE OF GOODS AND SERVICES

Yet, although services have become the major part of most economies, within the context of trade of goods and services, services have received much less attention than goods. What are the reasons for this? For one thing, they are hard to measure. Trade in manufactured goods is fairly straightforward. When a car that is made in Poland, or a Dior dress that is cut in Paris, or crates of McIntosh apples from the Okanogan Valley are exported and going through customs, they are easily recognized, classified, and taxed. This type of measure is easily identified and compiled, and becomes hard data for economists who analyze the statistics.

But how do you quantify the professional guidance a life coach gives to his or her client? The amount of time spent? The results obtained? Not obtained? How do you measure the time, knowledge, and value a doctor or a lawyer provides to give you a diagnosis or advice? By the time these professionals spent in school? By the number of people on their staff? By the amount of their bill? What about call centers? How do you measure the services that they render? Yet according to Ed Black (2012), Tech Association CEO, significantly more people work in the *engineering services* sector in the United States than work in the *production* of cars and automotive parts, and three times the number of people in the United States are employed in the "computer systems design engineering" sector than in the entire field of aerospace manufacturing.

Services often stay uncounted and therefore are not reported. It is therefore indispensable to be clear as to what a service is, and how it is defined in our economies. Since more than two-thirds of the world's economy is dealing with services, this is certainly worth looking at.

## PRODUCTS AND SERVICES AND THEIR DIFFERENCES

The differentiation between goods and services was first articulated by Adam Smith in his famous book, *The Wealth of Nations*, published in Great Britain in 1776. He defined the results of what he considered "productive" and "unproductive" labor. Productive labor produced goods that could be stored after production as saleable goods and then exchanged for money. Unproductive labor, such as that of the armed forces, clergy, lawyers, physicians, "men of letters," musicians, singers, buffoons, or "menial servants," which, "however honourable, ...useful, or ...necessary ...produce nothing for which an equal quantity of service can afterwards be procured, these services perished at the time of production ...therefore did not contribute to wealth." My, how times have changed! Daniel Pink, in his book *The Whole Mind*, describes how the MFA (Master of Fine Arts) is the new MBA, and that the arts and music are one of the biggest money-makers in our society.

We can look at products and services from the client's point of view.

*When a client asks "what can you make for me?" they are asking about products; when a client asks "what can you do for me?" they are asking about services. Whereas a product is something that can be measured and counted, a service is less concrete and is the result of the application of skills and expertise toward an identified need. A product is something you can point at, whereas a service, as The Economist defines it, is any activity "you can't drop on your foot," although this definition doesn't hold up when the products are digital in form—weightless objects that have no mass or material definition aside from tne physical media on which they exist. Nonetheless, even in file-based workflows, there is a distinction between a product being produced and a service provided to fill a need.*

**(The US National Archives and Records Administration)**

For example, digital file-based outputs can be digital files sent to a network storage system, new prints of motion picture film elements, prints for exhibit purposes, or reference copies on DVDs/CDs for reading rooms in libraries.

## THE PRODUCT-SERVICE CONTINUUM

Manufactured products today have a high service component. In the management literature this is referred to as the servitization of products. The old dichotomy between products and services is being replaced by a service-product continuum. Products and services are becoming more closely aligned and more and more products have a service element in them.

Many products come with a package of services that provide more continuous income than the sale of the product itself. GE's jet engine business sells the engines nearly at cost but bundles them with highly profitable, multiyear service contracts. IBM, even though it still manufactures computers, sees the manufacture of physical goods as a small part of its industry, with services becoming a major part of their business.

Adam Smith's comments on services being useless for the economy are past history. Companies that have invested in services, such as IBM, have shown that enormous profits are made as a result. IBM has been considered the gold standard in the services sector, and we will examine this further on.

A dramatic example of success coming from adding services is Boeing Aeronautics. Boeing went through a massive transformation over the past decade to become a dynamic services leader. Of course, Boeing still builds airplanes. But it has also expanded into the services business and operates with a global services-centric philosophy. So in addition to selling airplanes, spare parts and technical data, Boeing offers technical expertise and the rolling out of new platforms, supporting customers at their sites.

PetSmart, the pet food manufacturer, initiated a whole series of innovative services, including pet grooming, training, boarding, and other services, which account for a major share of its profits.

An excellent product no longer guarantees market success. The global marketplace has become highly competitive. Many businesses are shifting from selling products to providing service solutions and establishing good customer relationships.

Services have become—in their own way—"hot." What is not so clear is how to move an enterprise from a product-based to a service-oriented entity. How do services actually work—how are they created, how are they implemented, and how do they generate profits? Researchers are attempting to create a model for services success to help companies get started in this endeavor.

## ORGANIZATIONAL MODELS

Service businesses have traditionally used organizational models from the manufacturing sectors, incorporating notions such as hierarchy, task repetition, and standardization of procedures (Fragnière & Junod, 2010). The "Taylor model," used in the industrial sector, has also been used in the services sector. Fragnière and Junod maintain that this model has reached its limits, and is not appropriate nor useful in the service sector. Services use humans more than machines, so these production models can lead to organizational risks in the services sector. The authors state that analyzing knowledge-based services is more complex than the mechanistic approach to producing tangible products. As stated earlier, services are intangible and heterogeneous. The "production" of services is based on human soft skills, a contractual agreement between the provider and the client, and not assembly line procedures. The raw material is knowledge, not physical things.

We can appreciate the challenge—how do we make a science out of the intangible and the invisible? That is one reason that Service Science is so interesting—it seeks to materialize that which remains an interaction in a particular time, in a particular space, between two or more entities for the benefit of both.

## RISK FACTORS

Catenazzo and Fragnière (2011) have written about the risks taken in managing the invisible. This invisible process, which is the exchange between human beings, entails a risk factor. They give the example of a waiter handling clients in a restaurant. One client is alone, stressed and in a hurry to eat; the other is ordering the same pizza, but is accompanied by a friend, is content to eat at a leisurely pace, and is happy to be there. The manner in which the two clients are served would have to be quite different. A good waiter (*serveur* in French) would size up the situation, intuitively gauging the psychological and sociological factors, mood, and disposition, and anticipating the clients' needs.

Service providers have no choice but to interact positively with clients in order to augment customer satisfaction and reduce the risk of dissatisfaction. (We have all lived the exact opposite of this theory.) Negative appraisals of service are more harmful for services than for physical products. One solution to diminish the risk factor in services is the necessity for knowledge sharing between experienced staff and beginners in order to improve the quality of a service.

> ...*successfully managing the risks involved in service provision mean always "keeping your eye on the ball" during the process (e.g., during the conception,*

*during the production, and during the conclusion). Just like an artisan, the delivery of the service uses equal parts expertise and experience to assure real-time perfect execution. Knowledge acquired over time will permit increased value-added in the eyes of the clients, and can reduce the inherent risks of dissatisfaction and a bad reputation that are related to the delivery of an "invisible" good.*

**Catenazzo and Fragnière (2011)**

## THE CONTACT FACTOR

A service engenders a *client-based relationship*, a factor of prime importance. We require our family doctor to be a person who cares, who listens, who is of good counsel, and someone we like and trust. We have a relationship with him or her that lasts for decades, and we miss his or her presence when he or she retires. The same perhaps exists with other professionals who provide us with their specialized services. We refer our family and friends to these service providers who then maintain long-term satisfying customer relationships. Normally people do not change their providers specifically because of this special relationship, even when the service could cost less elsewhere. The human factor, complex and beautiful as it is, is an important, if not the most important element in the rendering of a service that will survive over time. If you are selling a service, you are also selling a relationship.

Customer contact is of prime importance in service operations. For example, high customer contact services would include those received in health centers, or from individuals with specialized knowledge, such as the architect who designs your home with you, or the consultant who designs a team-building seminar for your business, the lawyer who wins your case or the pediatrician who treats your child.

We find lower customer contact in areas that provide services such as the local branch of your post office, your bank, or the retail stores you frequent. Further down, a customer who has purchased an online airline ticket has little opportunity for involvement in the service delivery or communication with the provider, though contact can be made if necessary.

## SERVICE-DOMINANT VIEW

Vargo and Lusch (2004) have said that as the services sector has become dominant in most developed countries, they propose a different

marketing logic that is focused on a "service dominant" view revolving around three ideas. These notions are:
1. The co-creation of value, which maintains that the customer is the co-producer of the value of the service exchange.
2. The relationship with the customer, which is of prime importance; long-term relationships allow better adaptation of the service offerings to the needs of the customer.
3. The ability to meet the changes in demand while retaining service quality, and that the quality of service is determined by the customer.

An organization that adopts a service-dominant logic will focus on selling a flow of service. It would determine the optimal configuration of goods for a level of service, the optimal organization needed to maintain the service, and the optimal payment mechanism in exchange for providing the service (Vargo & Lusch, 2004).

Another example could be an organization that has redefined its business from a company that sells a product such as automobile insurance to a service that is a "mediator of human trauma" (Henkoff, 1994). Henkoff describes the process of what happens when an accident occurs. Their team flies to the scene, gives support, and handles claims on the spot. Contact is made with 80% of accident victims within 9 hours. This approach has earned an automobile insurance company one of the highest margins in the property and casualty insurance industry, one which has notoriously low margins.

Social media is a game changer as far as the credibility of almost any service is concerned. Whether it's a pizzeria in Naples, a hotel in St. Moritz, a car rental in Athens, a safari in South Africa, horseback riding in Connemara, or a festival in Alaska, no service can afford to be less than its customers desire it to be. Because we will know whether it is good, and why, and whether it is bad, and why. And these reviews can make a difference as to a business thriving or bailing out.

The Economist Intelligence Unit (2013) published a report, The rise of the Customer-Led Economy, where they show that the customer is king again, and it is technology that has empowered them.

This would be a good section to recount some humorous examples of bad service; however, in the interests of space as well as upliftment, here is one example of good service, and giving credit where credit is due and the use of technology to make life easier: http://www.webcitation.org/6abBrVjaP.

## SELF-SERVICE

As advances in technology and a better understanding of how people interact occur, the methodology of delivering a service can change. The roles of the service provider and the customer and how they interact in the service delivery process can be redefined and expanded. An example is self-service. Activities that were once done by the service provider can be more efficient when done by the customer, such as checking in online, or eating at a self-service cafeteria, filling up at a self-service gas station, withdrawing money from an automated teller machine (ATM), going to a car wash, or buying books online.

Self-service grocery shopping is now so normal that we tend to believe it was always so. However, in the years prior to 1916, customers had to hand a list or talk to the clerk at the counter, who would fetch the items. The first self-service grocery store, with the unusual name of Piggly-Wiggly, was founded in Memphis, Tennessee in 1916. The concept of a store where customers served themselves was patented in 1917 by Clarence Saunders, and franchises sold to grocery chains. The first stores had turnstiles, check-out stands, and a few hundred items on shelves, each labeled with its price. Its success was tremendous, and other grocery chains caught onto the self-service wave in the 1920s and 1930s. Approximately 600 independently owned Piggly-Wiggly stores still exist in the midwestern and southern regions of the United States. Why the Name Piggly-Wiggly? We will never know. Saunders' reason is a mystery and has not been documented anywhere.

## SELF-SERVICE TECHNOLOGIES

Self-service technologies (SSTs) have changed the way a service provider interacts with customers and have also augmented the range and number of services offered.

Some examples of SSTs in use are:
- ATM
- Airline check-in
- Hotel check-in/out
- Car rental
- Betting machines
- Various vending services (food, drink, cameras, etc.)
- Tax preparation software
- Self-scanning at retail stores
- Internet banking
- Online auctions

- Package tracking
- Internet shopping (Amazon, Gap, etc.)
- Internet information search
- Distance learning/training

Self-service has become a way of life, saving resources and time, and giving the client a sense of independence and freedom.

Originally, service was seen as a value coming from the service provider to the customer, initiated by either one or the other. Classic provider–customer relationships created value by exchanging services. Services have become more complex and interdisciplinary with the increased growth and development of the service sector. There is a co-creation with both the provider and the customer, and this is an important part of service design. Value-in-use sees services as "shared and dynamic problem-solving endeavors that create value in multiple dimensions" (Wolfson, Tavor, & Shlomo, 2012).

New information, knowledge, and cutting edge technologies also changed the relationship between provider and customer. So the service boundary began shifting from a person-to-person service, to a service that is fully operated by the customer (self-service), and this has become generalized and common. This shift increases efficiency, because resources, time, costs, and physical effort are reduced. The customer enjoys greater access and flexibility, and gains more control, causing a shift of some of the responsibility to the customer.

## SUPER SERVICE

The shift can also go the other way—toward the provider—thus making the service a super service. In this case, it is the provider that does the activity normally done by the customer, such as personal shopping, or the service of a chef cooking in your home for a dinner party, or the delivery of a rental car to your home. There is a saving of time and effort for both the provider and customer. Other examples include online ordering of groceries and home delivery, banks that pay your bills, customer pick-up by airlines, stock inventories that are supplied by a provider, or hairdressers who come to your home. Cloud computing is the delivery of computing as a service rather than a product, whereby shared resources, software, and information are provided to computers and other devices as a utility (like the electricity grid) over a network, typically the Internet.

Super service is known as an activity if not by its name. The appellation of the concept is not as well known as that of service and self-service.

## SUSTAINABILITY AND SERVICES

Wolfson et al. (2012) have well explained the necessity for the sustainability of services, and how important it is to take this into account. They have published new models in this regard and their work should be seriously taken into consideration in any discussion of service provision. They maintain that if the heart of each service is its value, a sustainable service has two values: its core value and the super value, which is co-created by the supplier and the customer. They cite as an example of a sustainable combination of self-service and super service the offering of free parking at the train station in order to encourage people to use their cars only to get to the train station. In addition people could bring their bicycles onto the train for use in the city center.

Redefining sustainability as a service—by definition an intangible product—shifts the focus from an economic profit point of view to one more concerned with environmental and social profits. It puts economics in this context, as an integral part of sustainability together with its environmental and social elements. Economics thereby dovetails with the holistic philosophy of Service Science, which focuses on the whole operation and not only on its economic aspects.

But services are not entities unto themselves. They need to fit into a system or a function that is activated. They exist in systems that take on an identity of their own from both a functional and cultural point of view.

Having looked at service and services from many different angles, we now go to the next phase in this primer on Service Science—that of service systems.

## WHAT IS A SERVICE SYSTEM?

A service system is a dynamic configuration of resources: people, technology, organizations and shared information that creates and delivers value between the provider and the customer through service (IfM & IBM, 2008). Service systems have to use these resources in different modes in order to co-create value with customers. These resources are the building blocks of service systems, and the basic unit of analysis in Service Science is the service system.

This is where the notion of service systems provokes attention, for though the components are basic—people, technology, organizations, and information—the way they are put together, why, and how, impact daily life as we know it today.

> *Every day we're customers of about 40 different types of service systems in the world: from the minute we wake up and turn on the lights, the electric service; to when we drive or take the bus to work, transportation services; to when we pick up our morning coffee, our retail service; there's just a huge number of service systems that we depend on for our quality of life these days.*
>
> *Spohrer (2009a)*

So what constitutes a service system? First of all, of course, people—who are they; how many are involved; what do they think, talk about, do?

Second, the technology involved—what type is used, what processes are engendered? What is the infrastructure of the technology? What hardware and equipment are being used? What software? What mode is being used in the buildings, their vehicles for transportation? What tools are made available?

Third, the aspect of shared information—what is everyone expected to know, have access to? What language, norms, beliefs, and attitudes are expected? Which laws and regulations, policies and instructions are put in place? What rules and procedures, plans and flowcharts are being followed? Which software and applications are being used, for what purpose?

The fourth component, organizations, are nonphysical resources that are formal, that is, legal entities that can contract and own property; for example, businesses, government agencies, banks, insurance companies, and suppliers. They can also be informal, such as temporary project teams, working groups, or web communities.

Value propositions,—that is, what is being valued, what is the division of labor, what is the risk factor, what safeguards are put in place—encompass the entire system.

## SYSTEMS AND FUNCTIONS

There are three broad categories of service systems, which then break down into specific functions. There are certainly more than those listed, but this gives the general idea, as listed in the IBM University Relations Worldwide Community Wiki.

The first broad category of service systems are the systems that focus on the flow of services that people need to survive, basic needs such as:
- Transportation
- Water and waste recycling
- Food and products manufacturing
- Energy and electricity

- Information and communication technology access

The second broad category are the systems that focus on human activity and development:
- Buildings and construction
- Retail and hospitality
- Banking and finance/Business and consulting
- Health and family life
- Education and work life

And the third broad category are the systems that focus on human governance:
- Cities and security for families and professions
- States/regions and commercial development opportunities
- Nations/NGO's and citizen's rights/rules/incentives/policies/law

The provision of the services found in these systems meets the routine daily needs for society. Every day we interact with dozens of service systems. A family or even an individual can be viewed as a service system, as can a city, a country, a government, or a company. Universities are designed service systems, so are hospitals. Service systems may be nested inside of other service systems; for example, staff and an operating room unit inside a hospital that is part of a nationwide health care provider network. A service system can be likened to the big picture—with separate distinct components, links, and connections to other service systems or to other services. The picture of a cruise ship is a good example of a service system—a literal floating city that provides for every basic, wellness, and entertainment need of its temporary inhabitants.

The smallest service system is a single person and the largest service system is the world economy. Service systems can be characterized by the value that results from the interaction between service systems, whether the interactions are between people, businesses, or nations. The interaction could take place between two technological systems and be performed through web services. It could be that people in one system are interacting with technology in another as in business-to-consumer e-commerce. Finally, it could be that technology is mediating people-to-people interactions such as when a researcher interacts through chat or e-mail with a reference librarian to find information.

Of course, the language, norms, attitudes, and beliefs of the people that make up a service system evolve and change over time. In this sense, service systems are a type of complex system that is partially designed and partially evolving.

Service systems can be divided into *front office* and *back office*, also called *front stage* and *back stage*, terms that are well known to the information scientist. The *front office* is about customer interaction, the service provider giving the service to the customer, ensuring customer satisfaction. The *back office* is about operational functions—the infrastructure in the background that ensures all the elements are present for the efficient running of the service. Service performance relies on both *front office* and *back office* components. The customer's participation as well as his feedback is an important part of the choreography.

## HOLISTIC SERVICE SYSTEMS

A holistic service system is defined as "a service system that can support the people within it, with some level of (1) completeness (quality of life associated with whole service), (2) independence (from all external service systems), and (3) extended duration (longer than a month if necessary and in some cases indefinitely)." A holistic service system can be a nation, state, city, university, hospital, cruise ship, family, or household, which provides whole service to the people inside the holistic service system (Spohrer, Fodell, & Murphy, 2012).

A great deal is known about luxury resort hotels within the Service Science community, so this provides a good foundation for future research on whole service and holistic service systems. Universities are important types of holistic service systems in an accelerating knowledge economy. Universities are mini-cities, and can become the laboratories for much of the research on whole service.

A luxury cruise ship is another good example of a holistic service system. Holistic service systems can remain viable for some period of time, even if disconnected from all interactions with other external service systems for an indefinite period of time.

## SERVICE SYSTEMS EXPAND

Service systems form a growing proportion of the world economy and are becoming central to the way businesses, governments, families, and individuals work. Innovation, a term applied almost exclusively to technologies in the past, is increasingly used in relation to service systems (IfM & IBM, 2008). Just as computer scientists work with formal models of algorithms and computation, service scientists are beginning to work with formal models of service systems.

Sustainability is an intangible product that requires the integration of a wide variety of knowledge, technologies, methods, and skills, and thus readily lends itself to being defined as a service system within the framework of Service Science. Considering sustainability as part of Service Science will enable us to understand it from a novel, more well-defined, practical point of view and will delineate its space of action while generating a new tool box for operation (Wolfson et al., 2012).

These basic services and the systems in which they live, with which we are all familiar, are the basis of new ways of thinking and analyzing, and provide new frontiers for research and discovery.

> A fair number of our interactions with specific service systems did not exist twenty years ago, before internet and mobile wireless technology, even fewer of those available today existed one hundred years ago before instantaneous global communications and social-institutional changes such as women joining the workforce in large numbers. We need to better understand how we got here, and what opportunities exist for where we might be going. Social, technological, economic, environmental and political changes are all interdependent. How can we get smarter simultaneously along all these dimensions?
> 
> *Spohrer (2009b)*

How can we get smarter, indeed? Service Science is pushing with dynamic forward motion for a full view of a topic that consists of many individual topics. It insists on bringing them together for a common goal.

## SERVICE SYSTEMS IN INFORMATION WORK

Information centers in any discipline and libraries are the service system base for the work of the information and knowledge professional.

In attempting to discuss Service Science with information professionals, I found that most think that Service Science is about managing information services! Needless to say, this further fueled my resolve to write this book. It is not my intention to discuss the management of information services, however the References section does include references that are pertinent to this area.

In the 1998 edition of his now classic textbook, *Foundations of Library and Information Science*, Richard Rubin wrote that service is the raison d'être of a library. In the third edition of the book, published in 2010, he examined the services that developed because of the impact of the Internet, the World

Wide Web; blogs, wikis, and other forms of social networking, as well as library services such as roving reference, e-government, and gaming.

At the same time, one of the purposes of the book, described by the author in the preface, is:

> *To place Library and Information Science in a larger social, economic, and political context. It is too easy to view the work of LIS professionals purely within an institutional setting. Increasingly, librarians and other information professionals must negotiate and respond to a variety of political, economic, technological, and social forces.*
>
> *Rubin (2010)*

To support this, one study that is interesting from an ethnographic perspective (Bouthillier, 2000) was designed to understand public library service in relation to social and historical issues. Bouthillier states that if service is the raison d'être of a library, the details of service provision are rarely seen as interconnected with social issues. However, "librarianship evolved in relation to the development of a certain service ideal … tied to culture, history and society."

Her discussion of how library services developed (or rather didn't develop) in Quebec compared to Anglophone Canada, and indeed to the rest of the world, is an important reflection on the necessity of an ethnographic optique in services.

> *Librarianship evolved in relation to the development of a certain service ideal, and the problems associated with it have been expressed in the library literature for many decades. This study, however, simply illustrates with empirical evidence that the problems encountered in the materialization of this service ideal do not belong exclusively to the domain of public libraries and librarians because they are tied to what goes on in culture, history, and society.*
>
> *Bouthillier (2000)*

Bouthillier's study is landmark research in services in information in this context.

Flash forward to 2012, where a professor of Service Science teaches students how to do service design using ethnomethodology, and describes the need for a full scope of cultural, operational, and experiential contexts when designing a service. Whereas Bouthillier wrote about the materialization of the service ideal, Fragnière, Nanchen, and Sitten (2012) use the word tangibilize, which takes the social codes and systems of beliefs that drive the service experience. The results of his service design study using an information service in a Swiss ski resort can be applied to other services, having found a model that he teaches in a Service Science lab. Both authors are saying that services, which involve both a provider and a client, need to be situated in the cultural, historical, social, and operational context of both the provider, whether it is a library, or any other type of service, and the client. This too is Service Science.

## LIBRARY 2.0 AND THE LONG TAIL

The idea of adapting and changing and learning about environments in other contexts is not new to the information professional. Much has been written about Library 2.0, which advocates user-centered change. Casey and Savastinuk (2006), describe Library 2.0 as a model for service that invites user participation for the virtual and physical services they want in the next generation library, and to reach new users rather than targeting clients we already have.

However, the authors maintain that libraries are in the habit of providing the same services and the same programs to the same groups. Little attention is paid to the greater part of the population that never uses library services. These authors encourage information professionals to make use of what Chris Anderson, then the editor-in-chief of *Wired*, called "the long tail" (Anderson, 2004). Anderson later published a book called *The Long Tail: Why the Future of Business Is Selling Less of More*, (Anderson, 2006), and a Smarter Comics version in 2011. Casey and Savastinuk maintain that no matter how hard we try, many of the services we offer are not being used by the majority of our users. Libraries are constrained by physical space and by money, and cannot handle every item that every user wants.

The long tail is a modernized version of Pareto's 80/20 rule. Anderson observed that only 20% of films will be released onto the mass market, and only 20% of these will be hits. Anderson uses the long tail to describe online businesses such as Amazon and Netflix, which thrive on selling fewer of a large variety of objects to more people.

Anderson gives a wonderful example of the phenomenon of the long tail concerning a book about a dangerous mountain climbing experience. *Touching the Void* by Joe Simpson was almost out of print when 10 years later a book on a similar topic, *Into Thin Air*, by Jon Krakauer, hit the best-seller lists. Suddenly *Touching the Void* began selling again. Why? Amazon.com recommendations, and positive public opinion reviews. *Touching the Void* became such a best seller it outpaced *Into Thin Air*, came out in a paperback edition, and was made into a docudrama. There was a rising demand for what had become an obscure book.

Anderson spoke about the long tail at one of the American Library Association's annual conferences, gave an interview for Ex Libris, and participated at a forum at the New York Public Library. There was obvious interest in this topic in the information professional community.

## HOW TO APPLY THE LONG TAIL TO INFORMATION WORK

Katherine Mossman (2006) gives an excellent explanation of how the long tail is pertinent for libraries in a list of eight lessons. Very briefly, they are:

1. Be responsive to your consumers in this highly competitive information marketplace, where proactive, innovative service is expected.
2. Locate the long tail of your community: the underserved and untapped. Develop creative outreach.
3. Find ways of solving all problems relating to access.
4. Go for being information filters rather than information brokers. Bring your expert guidance to an information marketplace that is "filled with junk."
5. You can compete with free—why libraries are not the first choice for information seekers.
6. The Internet (Google, Wikipedia, etc.) is both our competitor and not our competitor. If we could define where we fit with this technology, we'd be better positioned to improve our services, our products, and therefore our market position.
7. Capitalize on all types of service points, real and virtual, to the patron-consumer's greatest end. Let go of our taxonomies based on nineteenth century subject headings.
8. Using Google for research is not worth it. "Libraries will regain market position when we deliver more than Google can."

Admittedly, libraries are not profitmaking entities that now need to look for market niches in the long tail. Mossman maintains,

> Although libraries don't strive for profit, they wouldn't have survived all this time if all they had offered were the Danielle Steels and John Grishams of the publishing landscape. Through their own deep, historical collections and far-reaching services ... libraries can offer their customers access to an extensive number and variety of materials.

The advent of Library 3.0 is no reason we should ignore the very useful and still relevant principles described in Library 2.0.

## LIBRARY 3.0

Library 3.0 promises an even wider range of action for the information professional. Tom Kwanya, Christine Stilwell, and Peter Underwood (2015) have recently published an exciting volume titled *Library 3.0: Intelligent Libraries and Apomediation.*

This title analyzes Library 3.0 and its potential in creating intelligent libraries capable of meeting contemporary needs, and the growing role of librarians as apomediators. According to the book description on *Science Direct*, it "focuses on social media in research and academic libraries, gives context to the discussion of apomediation in librarianship and information services provision, and provides a balance between more traditional and more progressive approaches." This approach is definitely one to watch as it deals with user-centered information services for an emerging generation and it shows how to move toward 3.0.

## THE KNOWLEDGE ECONOMY AND LIFE-LONG LEARNING

Not all learning happens in academia. For example, the public library is a service system that has its place and role in the knowledge economy, especially in the context of lifelong learning.

The Carnegie public libraries played a major educational role in the transition from the agricultural to the industrial economy over one hundred years ago. One could make a case that they are now called upon to play a similar educational role in the transition from the industrial to the emerging knowledge economy.

> *In the past, our stocks of knowledge, - what we know, - was a great source of economic value. Because of the increasing rate of change, the real economic value has now moved from the stocks of knowledge to the flows of new knowledge that we are now able to quickly acquire...*
>
> *Economic value, for individuals as well as institutions, has thus been shifting from the amount of knowledge we have acquired over the years, to our ability to constantly learn. It is within this context that one has to consider the value of social networks and institutions, like libraries, and their impact in helping people better connect with each other, and build sustaining relationships that enhance knowledge flows and innovation.*
>
> *As the Web continued to evolve toward its Web 2.0, social networking phase, these new social networking capabilities have reminded us that humans are inherently social. We get together, establish communities and work and play as a team. We organize into a wide variety of institutions to get things done more effectively. We like to communicate, share ideas and learn from each other.*

> *The library's role as the physical, intellectual centre of the community is important in this new era. With its many public events, - talks, panels, discussions, and so on, - the library provides an environment where people can physically interact with each other in an intellectually stimulating environment... The community library is becoming one of the key places where adults can learn about and keep up with the latest digital tools and, in particular, how to best use them to access information and participate in social media activities. Given the importance of lifelong learning, the library can teach us how to leverage these powerful digital tools for both individual and group education*
> 
> *Wladawsky-Berger (2011)*

The systems and the methodologies in which we work are part of the landscape that Service Science spans. The following section is a brief look at a relatively unknown service system, with a wide scope in terms of geography, language, and culture in the international sector.

## THE INTERNATIONAL INFORMATION SECTOR

Information professionals working in service systems in the international sector are cognizant of the cultural, social, and economic contexts of their users in all parts of the world. They have a very wide scope within which they work. They are expected to provide information to high-powered research institutes, universities, and the private sector that need their highly specialized expertise and knowledge. At the other end of the spectrum they serve people or institutions that need information but still do not have connectivity, and so this information must be provided by other means.

For example, the World Health Organization Library and Information Networks for Knowledge Department, in response to the plea for health information from the least developing countries, decided to provide basic health care manuals to places where there were no computers or libraries, or even health clinics. The WHO information specialists and medical experts selected precious primary health care manuals, books, and articles that contained basic material such as how to set a broken arm, or how to treat an infant who had diarrhea, or how to use mosquito nets to avoid malaria. This material was placed in a blue metal trunk equipped with two shelves that could house about 100 books. The trunks are impervious to changing weather conditions and shipped to districts in Africa, and later to other regions. These trunks were named Blue Trunk Libraries (http://www.webcitation.org/6abCioG7J).

The initiative was highly successful, and thank-you's were received from health workers who had walked several miles to a phone in order to express their gratitude. This program is still going strong, with trunks going out to different regions in English, French, Arabic, Spanish, and Portuguese.

## RESEARCH4LIFE

This type of material was not necessary in the cities, where there were universities and libraries and hospitals. This was a different context—here researchers and students and doctors, although they had access to computers, could not meet the enormous costs of the online medical journals that they desperately needed. In answer to this need, the WHO Library came up with an ingenious plan to convince the publishers of these journals to allow free access to countries below a certain GDP. The argument was that the publishers did not have clients in these areas anyway, and probably never would. So why not share the world's medical knowledge with a sector that had so much need for it? One by one the major publishers agreed, and HINARI Access to Research in Health was born.

Three other international organizations, The Food and Agriculture Organization (FAO), the United Nations Environmental Programme (UNEP), and the World Intellectual Property Organization (WIPO) decided they wanted the same access for their areas of expertise and joined WHO in a collective program that was named Research4Life, (2015).

HINARI (Access to Research in Health) was joined by AGORA (Access to Global Online Research in Agriculture), OARE (Online Access to Research in the Environment), and ARDI (Access to Research for Development and Innovation); these Research4Life programs provide developing countries with free or low-cost access to academic and professional peer-reviewed content online. Research4Life is a public—private partnership of the WHO, FAO, UNEP, WIPO, Cornell and Yale Universities, and the International Association of Scientific, Technical & Medical Publishers.

This illustrates systems within systems, with service moving the gift of the world's knowledge from one system to another for mutual benefit.

## THE BIGGER PICTURE

I would like to end this chapter with a quote from Joseph Janes, Associate Professor at the Information School, University of Washington, Seattle, who wrote the foreword to Rubin's book *Foundations of Library and Information Science*. He describes the study of information as:

> ...also the story of humanity. Look at the sweep of human history and what you will find is the records and traces: cave drawings, scrolls, clay tablets, manuscripts, books, newspapers, pamphlets, journals, diaries, letters, paintings, sound recordings, moving images, blogs, and on and on and on. From Lascaux to YouTube, the message is the same: I was here, and I have a story to tell.
>
> *Rubin (2010)*

All of this is to say that the information professional is by definition obliged to be in and ahead of the environment in which he or she works. Therefore the case for knowing about Service Science....

Next we will explore the fascinating story of Service Science, how it was born, and what it is about.

## REFERENCES

American Marketing Association Committee on Definitions (1960). *Marketing definitions: A glossary of marketing Terms*. Chicago: AMA.
Anderson, C. (2004). The long tail. *Wired*, Issue 12.10, October 2004.
Anderson, C. (2006). *The long tail: Why the future of business is selling less of more*. New York, NY: Hyperion.
Baruch, J. J., Quinn, J. B., & Cushman Paquette, P. (1987). Technology in services. *Scientific American, 257*(2), 50.
Black, Ed. (2012). <http://www.webcitation.org/6abGOecyb> Accessed April 2015.
Bouthillier, F. (2000). The meaning of service: ambiguities and dilemmas for public library service providers. *Library and Information Science Research, 22*(3), 243−272, ISSN: 0740-8188.
Bryson, J. R., Daniels, P. W., & Warf, B. (2004). *Service worlds: People, organizations, technologies*. New York, NY: Routledge, (p. 33).
Casey, M. E., & Savastinuk, L. C. (2006). Service for the next-generation library. *Library Journal, 131*, 40, 1 September.
Catenazzo, G., & Fragnière, E. (2011). Managing the risks of the "invisible". *Service Science, 3*(3), i−iv.
the Economist. *Economics A to Z*. <http://www.economist.com/economics-a-to-z/s#node-21529672> Accessed April 2015.
the Economist Intelligence Unit. (2013). *The rise of the customer-led economy*. <http://www.webcitation.org/6abI0psnT> Accessed April 2015.
Fitzsimmons, J. A., & Fitzsimmons, M. J. (2005). *Service management: Operations, strategy, and information technology* (4th ed.New York, NY: McGraw-Hill.
Fragnière, E., & Junod, N. (2010). The emergent evolution of human risks in service companies due to control industrialization: an empirical research. *Journal of Financial Transformation, 30*, 169−177.
Fragnière, E., Nanchen, B., & Sitten, M. (2012). Performing service design experiments using ethnomethodology and theatre-based reenactment: a Swiss ski resort case study. *Service Science, 4*(2), 89−100.
Glückler, J., & Hammer, I. (2011). A pragmatic service typology: capturing the distinctive dynamics of services in time and space. *The Service Industries Journal, 31*(6).

Gronroos, C. (1990). *Service management and marketing.* Lexington, MA: Lexington Books.

Henkoff, R. (1994). Service is everybody's business. *Fortune, 129*(13), 49.

Hill, T. P. (1977). On goods and services. *The review of income and wealth, 23*(4), 314–339. <http://www.webcitation.org/6abIKfM6g> Accessed April 2015.

IBM University Relations Worldwide Community. <http://www.webcitation.org/6abIY4KOV> Accessed April 2015.

IfM and IBM (2008). *Succeeding through service innovation: A service perspective for education, research, business and government.* Cambridge, UK: University of Cambridge Institute for Manufacturing.

Krakauer, J. (1999). *Into thin air.* New York, NY: Anchor Books.

Kwanya, T., Stilwell, C., & Underwood, P. (2015). *Library 3.0: Intelligent libraries and apomediation.* Chandos.

Lovelock, C., & Gummesson, E. (2004). Whither services marketing? In search of a new paradigm and fresh perspectives. *Journal of Service Research, 7*(1), 20–41.

Maglio, P. P., Kieliszewski, C. A., & Spohrer, J. C. (2010). *Handbook of Service Science.* New York, NY: Springer.

Mossmann, K. (2006). Serving the niche. *Library Journal,* 38–40, 7/06.

Ostrom, A. L., Parasuraman, A., Bowen, D. E., Patricio, L., & Voss, C. A. (2015). Service research priorities in a rapidly changing context. *Journal of Service Research, 18*(2), 127–159. <http://www.webcitation.org/6abJ2kfDI> Accessed April 2015.

Pink, D. (2005). *A whole new mind.* New York, NY: Riverhead Books.

Research4Life. <http://www.webcitation.org/6abJWuEQL> Accessed April 2015.

Rubin, R. (2010). *Foundations of library and information science* (3rd ed.New York, NY: Neal-Schuman Publishers.

Simpson, J. (1988). *Touching the void.* New York, NY: Perennial.

Spohrer, J. (2009a). *How systems interact to deliver services.* <http://www.webcitation.org/6abJwzkAl> Accessed April 2015.

Spohrer, J. (2009b). Editorial column—Welcome to our declaration of interdependence. *Service Science, 1*(1), i–ii. <http://dx.doi.org/10.1287/serv.1.1.i>.

Spohrer, J., Fodell, D., & Murphy, W. (2012). Ten reasons Service Science matters to universities. *Educause Review, 47,* 6.

United Nations Department of Economic and Social Affairs. <http://www.webcitation.org/6abKGYslc> Accessed April 2015.

US National Archives and Records Administration. <http://www.webcitation.org/6abKmKAXX>, Accessed April 2015.

Vargo, S. L., & Lusch, R. F. (2004). Evolving to a new dominant logic for marketing. *Journal of Marketing., 68,* 1–17.

Wladawsky-Berger, I. 2011. *The Community Library in Our Emerging Knowledge Economy.* <http://www.webcitation.org/6abLOHptQ>.

Wolfson, A., Tavor, D., and Shlomo M. (2012). *Sustainability and shifting from a 'Person to Person' to a Super- or Selfservice.* <http://www.webcitation.org/6abM38dkp> Accessed April 2015.

Wordsworth, W. (1888). *The complete poetical works.* London: Macmillan and Co. Bartleby.com, 1999. <www.bartleby.com/145/> Accessed April 2015.

Zeithaml, V. L., & Bitner, M. J. (1996). *Services marketing.* New York, NY: McGraw-Hill.

# CHAPTER 2

# The Story of Service Science

*Everything, it seems, is interconnected and interdependent, and service is the glue that holds the world together.*

*Jim Spohrer, IBM*

## THE SHIFT TO A KNOWLEDGE ECONOMY

Though we are not going to go into an in-depth study of the economic history of the world (!) it is useful to look at the major world stages in order to position the knowledge economy in its logical place as part of the historical development of the economy. As information professionals I wonder if we appreciate our place and our role in this information economy, this knowledge economy. How amazing to find ourselves at the head of the parade. Information specialists in the information economy? Does it get any better? We always knew that information was the stuff the world was made of, and now economics proves this true. The universe has our back—how we lead with this is our challenge.

## AGRICULTURAL, INDUSTRIAL, AND POST-INDUSTRIAL ECONOMIES

The agricultural revolution began the world economy as we know it today. In an agrarian society the majority of the population lives and works on the land and produces its own food. The period between the eighteenth and nineteenth centuries saw food production expand because of advances in tools and machinery as well as farming practices, like crop rotation for example. Efficiency improved, and surpluses in food production could be sold for profit. Wealth was based on land ownership and what the land produced. During the agricultural phase, towns and cities grew, and regions began to deal in commerce and trade.

The industrial phase refers to the widespread creation of new industries, and more generally to the radical transformation of the economy from farming to manufacturing. The most famous industrial revolution occurred in Britain during the mid-eighteenth century and spread to the rest of Europe and the United States within a few decades. Russia, China, and India experienced theirs later, by the late twentieth century. The industrial society is one in which wealth is produced by turning raw materials into products that are sold in the marketplace. Wealth is based on capital.

The post-industrial, or the information or knowledge economy brings us to the present time. Whereas the agricultural and industrial phases were based on the production of goods, the post-industrial is rooted in information and services. We have a shift here from physical products to knowledge, ideas, and literacy, and the work force is an educated one.

## TYPES OF ECONOMIC SECTORS

We can also look at the five types of economic sectors: primary, secondary, tertiary, and the lesser known, quaternary and quinary, in order to see what percentage of the population is engaged in which sector of activity. These categories show the relative distance moved from the natural environment.

It starts with the primary sector, which is that part of the economy that uses products from the earth, including basic foods, and the production of raw materials along with their packaging and processing. Activities that are part of the primary sector include agriculture, farming, forestry, mining, quarrying, fishing, and hunting. In the mid-nineteenth century two-thirds of the labor force in America were primary sector workers, compared to 3% today. In both developed and developing countries the number of workers in this sector are decreasing.

The secondary sector is the manufacture of finished products. Manufacturing, processing, and construction are all part of the secondary sector. Activities in this sector include construction, automobile production, textile production, metal working and smelting, the chemical and engineering industries, energy utilities, aerospace manufacturing, shipbuilding, and breweries.

The tertiary sector of the economy is the service industry, providing services to the population and to business. Activities include everything we have seen so far as services, including retail sales, transportation and distribution, entertainment, restaurants, tourism, insurance, health care, banking, legal, and clerical as a few examples. In all developed countries and some developing countries the biggest proportion of workers are now in the tertiary sector.

Some economists also describe the quaternary and quinary sectors. The quaternary is largely found in work that consists of intellectual activities. These include work dealing with education, scientific research, government, culture, libraries, and information technology.

The quinary sector is sometimes considered a branch of the quaternary sector. This sector deals with the highest level of decision making in a society. It includes the top level officials in, for example, government, science, health care, culture, the media, and universities.

## THE ECONOMIC IMPORTANCE OF SERVICES

As early as the 1970s the emerging patterns of the service economy were being studied in terms of their economic importance and impact on employment. Service activities were springing up inside and outside of industries. By the end of the 1970s the service economy was being understood as a fait accompli, and the dichotomy between industry and services was being replaced by an integration—that services are the key to better industry and production.

The 1973 economic crisis was particular in that wealth production had changed, and services became the major player. Economic theories that had been applied to industrial manufacturing were woefully inadequate in explaining the new reality. At the same time, services were given an official status at the international negotiations level of the Uruguay Round of talks. An economic theory of services was being called for as the industrial economy began shifting to a service economy.

Previously in the industrial society services were not as important and had a secondary role. However, it was becoming clear that for each product, complex service and delivery work had to take place. The service economy was not necessarily replacing the industrial one, it was simply the result of forward motion, supplemented by technology and a change in the value system. Services represented the next stage of the development of economic history, and dovetailed with manufacturing in the same way that industry had dovetailed with the agricultural economy in earlier times.

*Through industrialization, directly or indirectly, agriculture has become more efficient. And now both agriculture and manufacturing industry have more and more to rely on the development of services in order to ameliorate their economic performance in production and distribution.*

*FEMDI (1991)*

There are several functions in which services are key in the production of wealth. Research and development services occur long before production takes place, as do market research studies, and service functions such as planning, maintenance, storage, and quality control. Distribution is a service, and is key for both products and services. Teaching people how to use products is another service. Industrial production creates waste and pollution, and services are the means to deal with this.

Critics of the service economy say that products are still the major player in the economy, and that without products, there would be no services. Two hundred years ago, the critics of the industrial revolution said the same thing in terms of industry being impossible without agricultural products, with industrialization being secondary.

> It is obvious that agriculture and manufacturing industry are essential, and that one cannot simply forget them: but today it is also true that any sort of product which does not rely on the functioning of services is simply not in a condition to be used or even produced. Products of any sort can only exist economically through the service system.
>
> *FEMDI (1991)*

## THE SERVITIZATION OF BUSINESS

Sandra Vandermerwe and Juan Rada, of the (then) International Management Institute in Geneva, coined the term "servitization of business." They described how corporations were adding value to their products through services, thus sharpening their competitive edge. Corporations were adding bundles of goods, services, support, self-service, and knowledge to their market packages, thus forging new relationships with their customers.

> It is no longer valid for either industries or individual corporations to draw simplistic distinctions between goods and services or assume they can do one without the other. Most firms today, are to a lesser or greater extent, in both. Much of this is due to managers looking at their customers' needs as a whole, moving from the old and outdated focus on goods or services to integrated "bundles" or systems, as they are sometimes referred to, with services in the lead role.
>
> *Vandermerwe and Rada (1988)*

The servitization of business developed in stages. First it was goods OR services, and companies were either in one or the other. With the coming of advanced technologies, it was clear that companies needed to do one AND the other, computer manufacturers being early examples of the inseparability of products and services. Finally, the equation began looking like goods + services + support + knowledge + self-service. In this instance, support can be training, maintenance, co-producing services, new set-ups. Knowledge is more than information—it is the cumulative know-how and experience of the company used for individual tailor-made solutions for customers.

## THE RISE OF THE SERVICE SECTOR

Service Science is coming into being because of the service sector's spectacular rise to dominate today's economy. The manufacturing of physical products peaked in the United States in the mid-1950s and has been decreasing ever since. The service sector began to outnumber and outweigh the other sectors in the United States and other parts of the world, and thus became the main and fastest growing phenomenon in most economies (Figure 2.1).

In 2010 the service sector generated more than 70% of the GDP in most advanced economies, including the United States, Canada, Australia, Japan, 10 countries in the European Union, and Switzerland. Brazil (67%), Russia (59%), India (55%), and China (43%) are not far behind in these figures (International Monetary Fund, April 2011). The growth of services is expected to continue to rise in all countries.

## REASONS FOR THE SHIFT

There are several main reasons for the growth of the service sector in the major economies of the world (Lovelock, Wirtz, & Chew, 2009). For one thing, automation increased productivity in agriculture and industry, therefore the percentage of people working in related services increased continuously. There was also a growing demand for new services. International trade and tourism resulted in a demand for the transportation of people as well as things. International finance, communications, hotels, and food services expanded around the world. People could spend more on services as their standard of living went up. Functions we used to do ourselves could now be hired out to other people. There was more time and more money to take vacations, to be entertained, to go to restaurants. Also, services gave a new perspective in terms of benefits accrued without the responsibility of ownership. Rented

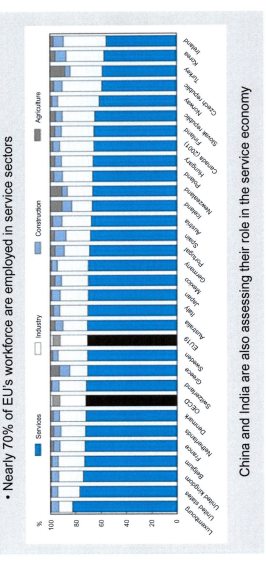

Figure 2.1 Services offer significant economic opportunities.

services provided the temporary right to use a particular good, space, labor, or expertise.

We began paying proportionately more for services in the form of experience, advice, information, assurance, infrastructure, and learning, and proportionately less on growing, building, and owning physical goods (IfM & IBM, 2008). Companies began to see the advantages of outsourcing internal services, for example payroll administration, or office cleaning, or landscape maintenance to subcontractors. All of these tasks became part of the services component of the economy.

At the same time markets were shifting to service economies, there was an increasing use of information technology in traditional service areas, including utilities, building maintenance, retail, hospitality, finance, health, education, and government. The result was that the service sector became more knowledge intensive and required more technical skills. Technology alone has resulted in the creation of entire new service industries such as Amazon and Google and the rapid emergence of social computing tools. "New information technologies have constituted a technological and industrial revolution in service provisioning..." (IfM and IBM, 2008).

These changes are global, they affect everyone. In fact, the economies of the world are becoming one large service system. The growth in service jobs parallels the growth of the knowledge economy, in both developed and developing countries. The International Labour Organization (2007) reported that for the first time, as far back as 2006, more people worked in the service sector *worldwide* than in either the manufacturing or agricultural sectors. The bottom line is that the service sector is where the job growth is, around the world.

## IN TANDEM WITH THE SHIFT?

Graduates around the world were entering an economy with jobs to a large degree in the service sector. Were they equipped to do so? No, they were not. Were the public and private sectors getting the type of employee they needed? Not always. There was no platform for the study and research of services. Programs to study service, service systems, and service innovation, especially in government, health care, and education, were sadly lacking. Many academic and government policy makers were still operating in a manufacturing paradigm rather than in a service paradigm. Scientists and engineers were being trained for jobs in the manufacturing sector.

A lively article by Jim Spohrer, Dianne Fodell, and Wendy Murphy (2012) in the Educause Review lists 10 reasons why Service Science matters to universities.

> Service Science can provide perspective on the forces reshaping higher education today. From online service offerings to self-service technologies to global brands establishing local franchises, these basic forces are transforming whole industries and are being studied by service scientists. Higher education is not the first industry to feel the tug of these forces, nor will it be the last, with finance, health care, and government on the horizon and with retail, media, manufacturing, and agriculture industries well down the road of twenty-first-century transformation in the age of global sourcing, cloud computing, and the "Internet of Things."

And with more than 24 academic disciplines teaching service from their own point of view, the need for a new transdiscipline, Service Science, becomes obvious (Rust & Huang, 2014).

Service Science is a concept that is a result of our time: a necessity in the knowledge economy. It is being born from the convergence of forces that are transforming the world, such as the continuous advancement of information technology, demographic shifts (for example an older, wealthier population in certain areas, and areas where the younger generation is over 50% of the total population), sustainability concerns, social change and globalisation, including the rise of the globally integrated enterprise. Global trends using web-based technologies, outsourcing and off-shoring are pushing us to create new ways of doing things.

These shifts — from the agricultural to the industrial to the knowledge economies – took only two hundred years. What is interesting is that we are no longer looking in the rear view mirror to describe a paradigm shift — we are actually living it, daily, and marvelling at the speed and intelligence of the change.

## TOWARD AN ECONOMY OF SERVICE AND KNOWLEDGE

Some thinkers could see the knowledge economy coming. In 1959 Peter Drucker wrote a book, *Landmarks of Tomorrow* (Drucker, 1959), in which he coined the term knowledge worker as the new emerging dominant group that would replace industrial workers. He believed that knowledge would replace raw material as the essential capital of the new economy. The term was virtually unknown then, but Drucker predicted that knowledge workers would become more than a third of the workforce in the United States. In fact, they became more than a third.

Later in his life Drucker[1] considered knowledge work productivity to be the next frontier of management. He considered this to be a liberal art that should derive lessons from many different areas; for example history, sociology, psychology, philosophy, culture, and religion. His controversial article, *The Age of Social Transformation*, published in the Atlantic Monthly of November 1994, speaks of the emerging knowledge society and what this implies in terms of jobs, education, lifelong learning, and social order. He describes how the farmer and the domestic worker in the agricultural economy could still shift into jobs in the industrial economy. However, it is not possible for the industrial worker to easily transition to knowledge work or services. The knowledge worker needs advanced formal education and the ability to apply theoretical and analytical knowledge. This is a different approach to work, and a different mind-set, one that requires continuous life-long learning.

A book titled *The Coming of Post-Industrial Society* was published in 1973 by Daniel Bell, a Harvard University sociologist. His theory was that jobs in knowledge-based services would overtake employment in manufacturing in a few decades. His predictions had come true by the year 2000. Over 70% of nonagricultural employment in the United States was in services and service-producing industries. The same was true in other developed nations.

Robert Reich, in *The Work of Nations: Preparing Ourselves for 21st Century Capitalism*, published in 1992, introduced economic theory in terms more suited to the information age. Reich re-examined the debate on the origins of wealth and postulated that in a knowledge-based economy wealth originated from a strong, innovative, and skilled work force.

Prusak and Davenport wrote the bestseller, *Working Knowledge: How Organizations Manage What They Know*, in 1998, and contributed another level of relevance of knowledge to business. In one of his blogs Prusak (2001) later wrote:

> Time becomes the currency in the knowledge economy, not money. It's because it's the way knowledge is manifested. It's because the form knowledge takes is in time. And time is what we don't have.

---

[1] A note to information professionals: To see what Drucker thought of librarians, go to http://www.ibiblio.org/slanews/conferences/sla2006/presentations/drucker.pdf.

Both academia and industry have been interested in the service sector since Adam Smith, but mainly from the point of view of marketing, management, and economics. However, with the advent of technology-enabled services, more and more revenue was being generated by service operations. Therefore service innovation began to be as important, perhaps even more important as innovation in technology. Yet, service innovation was generally unknown save for a few economists studying the relationship between investment and innovation in service industries.

Jim Spohrer, in an interview for this book says it this way. The interview question was: Besides IBM, are there other players, in both business and academia, that are also having an important impact on this emerging science today?

*Yes, there are several researchers and papers that describe this.*

*For the history of Service Science see: Spohrer, J. C., & Maglio, P. P. (2010). Toward a science of service systems. In* Handbook of Service Science *(pp. 157—194). Springer US.*

*For the future of Service Science see: The International Society of Service Innovation Professionals (http://www.webcitation.org/6acm9ozT0).*

*What I (Jim Spohrer) like to say is the following...*

*Service phenomena is as old as division-of-labour and role specialization in families. But the real explosion in formal service phenomena came with the invention of cities, written laws, and money.*

*Service research has a long history—at least since the time of (political economists) Adams, Ricardo, Bastiat, and then Colin Clark, William Baumol, Riordin (ATT systems engineering), Fuchs, etc in the sixties, but it really took off in Marketing and Operations in the 70's with the work at Harvard of Theodore Levitt... modern service research appeared in the Nordics with Christian Gronross's work, Evert Gummesson's work on relationship marketing and many to many networks, and in the US with the work of Mary Jo Bitner, Roland Rust, Ray Fisk, and many others—again Marketing and Operations—but in the 90's you see an explosion of Industrial and Systems Engineering (Tien & Berg, RPI and now Miami), Operations Research (Mendelson, Israel), and Computer Science (Service Computing, Service Oriented Architectures, Software as a Service, Web Services, and much, much more)... and also many governments began talking about service in the late 80's, 90's, and 00's... A big boost in the 2000's was the rise of Service-Dominant Logic by Vargo and Lusch.*

*What IBM did was "legitimize" the study of service systems from multiple disciplinary perspectives—with the name Service Science, Management, and Engineering and later SSME+D when Design was added—IBM said guess what—it is not just B2C service and Web Services, it is also B2B, and G2C, and B2G, etc.—all these service system entities are interacting to cocreate value*— *and we want to see "Service Science" become as important an area of study as the study of computers or computational systems... even later this evolved to SSME+DAPP (Service Science, Management, and Engineering+Design, Arts, and Public Policy), reflecting the fact that Service Science (the short name) was actually a transdiscipline, borrowing from many disciplines without replacing any of them).*

*Henry Chesbrough and I wrote the Service Science Manifesto to make this connection, and several other points in The Special Issue of the Communications of the ACM .*

*IBM wanted to understand service systems via Service Science, as well as we understood computational systems via computer science. Hopefully we accomplished several key things:*
- *amplified and integrated the multidisciplinary approaches to the study of service phenomena and approaches to service innovation*
- *suggested we (nations, businesses, universities) were long overdue in getting more systematic about the study of service phenomena*
- *said the focus should be on service systems (at all scales) and value-cocreation interactions (value propositions, governance)*

*And IBM said, Come on in, the water is fine:-)*

Because Jim has been involved with Service Science from the very beginning, his view of it as expressed in his words, is absolutely necessary at this point.

Now let's take a look at the story of how he managed to make it happen through IBM.

## THE IBM STORY

IBM has definitely played a major role in this amazing story of the birth of a new discipline. IBM had the need, as well as the means, the conviction, and the drive to call for a multidisciplinary approach to the study of services. IBM signaled the fact that nations, businesses, and universities were long overdue in establishing a systematic knowledge base for services that would be as important an area of study as that of computers and computational systems.

Dr. James C. Spohrer is Director, Global University Programs and Cognitive Systems Institute, at the IBM Almaden Research Center in San Jose, California. In 2004 Jim was setting up the IBM Research Service Department and he could not find job candidates with the right mix to work in his department. What he needed was a combination of knowledge in computer science, engineering, management, and social science. He complained about this to Henry Chesbrough, professor of business and innovation at Berkeley. Chesbrough reminded him that IBM had pushed forward computer science as a discipline by donating computers to universities and then helping them create curricula to teach students how to use the machines. "IBM started computer science. You should start Service Science," Chesbrough said to Spohrer. The two of them were so excited about the idea that they called Paul Horn, then director of IBM Research, who immediately approved the idea (IBM, 2010).

IBM had already lived through a major strategic shift to services in the 1990s by seeing how important it was to help clients deploy IT. It was the first to create an IT services business. In 2002 IBM acquired the consulting arm of PricewaterhouseCoopers to form the IBM Global Business Services, and IBM Research was the pioneer that created the field of Service Science. IBM now has 80% of its business in services and software, and reported record profits in 2010. "There was a huge shift from manufacturing to services," says Spohrer, "something big was happening in the world, and we had to deal with it." Spohrer maintains that the growth of the service sector of the economy is truly a wonder of human history, on a par with the agricultural revolution and the industrial revolution (Spohrer, 2011).

IBM began funding universities to help set up programs and research in Service Science, and it deployed some of its best brain power to promote, teach, and develop this young science. By 2006 IBM was investing $100 million a year, including grants and free access to IBM hardware and software to encourage universities to start building courses in Service Science, sometimes with the help of IBM staff, who often were adjunct professors.

Other businesses such as Cisco, Microsoft, Google, Oracle, Accenture, and Xerox are also promoting the Service Science concept by supporting professors, offering scholarships and internships, recruiting graduates, and offering research contracts, though not to the same degree as IBM.

In a *New York Times* interview in those early days (Holstein, 2006), Irving Wladawsky-Berger, who was then IBM's vice president for technical strategy and innovation and a visiting professor at MIT, was asked what IBM was doing on campus now. Wladawsky-Berger replied that because information technology was becoming embedded in all aspects of our lives, it was becoming necessary to focus on the people aspect of business, and that is what was meant by services. Since there were no universities with programs applying technology to the people aspect of business, IBM was working with universities around the world to help create this emerging discipline called Service Science.

When asked whether IBM was not simply looking for a commercial advantage, Wladawsky-Berger replied that many companies, as well as IBM, were working to a greater degree in services. People had to learn the basis of these processes and be prepared to innovate. He likened it to what happened in manufacturing 25 years ago: "Manufacturing is an example of how painful it is when a country does not take leadership in a particular area. I'm not sure that Detroit has ever recovered from that."

## GETTING STARTED

IBM has provided an abundant wealth of material on Service Science available online: wikis, modular courses, presentations on all aspects of Service Science, blogs, a community of practice, and more.

The IBM Global University Programs site has a wiki on Service Science that includes getting started, learning about, and teaching Service Science: https://www-304.ibm.com/connections/wikis/home?lang=en-us#!/wiki/IBM%20Global%20University%20Programs.

In the LEARN section of Getting Started you can get a comprehensive introduction to the subject of Service Science that includes a list of journals, the top 100 books in Service Science, a bibliography of books related to Service Science, and a recommended reading list.

In the TEACH section you can find a course materials page, case studies by industry, courses and lectures you can download, as well as other material to begin teaching.

The CONNECT section links to industry resources, University relations, government organizations that are mapping relevant Service Science issues, as well as expert resources, though this does not include all the movers and shakers in this field.

This is a good resource for looking at the history and evolution of Service Science ideas; however, we will look at how to keep up to speed with the current developments in later chapters.

## SERVICE SCIENCE

Service Science, also known as Service Science, Management, and Engineering (SSME), later as Service Science, Management, Engineering, and Design (SSME + D), and more recently as Service Science, Management, and Engineering + Design, Arts, and Public Policy (SSME + DAPP), is a discipline that began in the late 1990s and early 2000s. It is emerging; that is, the field is in the process of defining, describing, delineating, and agreeing on its content fully. Some would see this as chaos; others would see it as opportunity.

Service Science is the study of services, service systems, and value propositions. As discussed in Chapter 1, service systems are dynamic combinations of people, information, organizations, and technology that can create and deliver services. Value propositions are specific packages of benefits and solutions that a service system intends to offer and deliver to others. Service Science is the integration of many service research areas and service disciplines, including service economics, service marketing, service operations, service management, service quality, customer satisfaction, service strategy, service engineering, service human resource management, service computing service supply chain, service design, service productivity, and service measurement. Maglio and Spohrer (2008) define Service Science as "the study of service systems, which are dynamic value cocreation configurations of resources (people, technology, organizations, and shared information)."

The key to Service Science, as well as the challenge, is multidisciplinarity. It aims to focus on all aspects of service as a system of interacting parts. As such, Service Science draws on ideas from a number of existing disciplines and aims to integrate them into a coherent whole with its own identity.

When we take the four elements that make up a service system (people, technology, organizations, and information) and look at them through an academic lens, we can see which departments or disciplines have dealt with or deal with these elements. In general, people are studied in the social sciences and the humanities, technology is taught in schools of computer science and engineering, schools of management and business schools study organizations and how they are run, and information is taught in schools of information. And that is just the beginning of the multidisciplinary components in this new field.

*Service Science... is an emerging field. It includes curricula, training, and research programs that are designed to teach individuals to apply scientific, engineering, management and design disciplines that integrate elements of computer science, operations research, industrial engineering, business strategy, management sciences, social and legal sciences, and others in order to encourage innovation in how organisations create value for customers and stakeholders that could not be achieved through such disciplines working in isolation.*

**IfM and IBM (2008)**

To this list of disciplines can be added cognitive science, economics, organizational behavior, human resources management, marketing, communication, information science, and no doubt others. This has not yet been decided nor agreed upon.

Service Science has also been described as

*...an emerging interdisciplinary field of inquiry that focuses on fundamental science, models, theories, and applications to drive service innovation, competition, and well-being through co-creation of value. We view Service Science as encompassing many disciplines and perspectives that can contribute to our understanding.*

**Ostrom et al. (2010)**

*The Handbook of Service Science* (Maglio, Kieliszewski, & Spohrer, 2010) lays out the conceptual foundations of Service Science, including the list of terms every service scientist should know. The types of service system entities, their interactions with each other and the environment, plus their outcomes are what a service scientist studies. In addition, a fully refereed international journal, *Service Science* began, quarterly, online, with Paul Maglio as Editor-in-Chief.

Service Science is as important to the service sector and the knowledge economy as the foundation provided by physics, chemistry, biology, cognitive science, and computer science was for the agricultural and industrial eras.

## BASIC COMPONENTS

Service Science seeks to discover the basic building blocks of service systems and the value propositions that interconnect them. It attempts to provide the structure and rigor for building a coherent body of knowledge to support research and innovation in service systems and establish a common language.

These premises lead to questions that are fascinating to the service scientist. What are these basic building blocks of service systems, these blocks that lead to such variety? Can these building blocks help us understand the origins, life cycles, and sustainability of service systems? How can service systems be made to interact? Why do interactions within and between service systems lead to particular outcomes? Are these outcomes predictable? How can service innovation be stimulated, realized, and sustained?

For example, Steve Jobs made the choice to integrate Apple's hardware, software, content, design, retailing, management, company culture, and all services into one unified system. His genius was to build a company that was situated at the crossroads of art and technology, thus giving the world products and services that were new, that were beautiful, and once we had them, we knew we needed them.

An analogy can be made between Service Science and Computer Science. The success of Computer Science is not in the definition of a basic science (as in physics or chemistry, for example), but more in its ability to bring together diverse disciplines, such as mathematics, electronics, and psychology, to solve problems that require they all be there and talk a language that demonstrates common purpose. Service Science may be the same thing—just bigger—an interdisciplinary umbrella that enables economists, social scientists, mathematicians, computer scientists, and legislators (to name a small subset) to cooperate in order to achieve a larger goal.

It is a challenge to attempt an "umbrella" approach to knowledge, and to develop the capacity to think and act across multiple disciplines. Some would advocate the interdisciplinary approach, one that creates new knowledge to bridge and integrate many areas based on transdisciplinary and crossdisciplinary collaboration (IfM & IBM, 2008). This approach would acknowledge the barriers between disciplines and build bridges over them. In theory this appears to be a good approach. Interdisciplinary activities already exist in some universities and businesses.

However, specialization is the norm, and our entire academic and research funding structure is based on this. Academics are expected to teach and do research within their specialization area. It's just set up this way. Interdisciplinary research calls for new paradigms and methodologies and a mind-set that is open to other knowledge, and seeks to know how they link together and to their own specialization. What is required is a new attitude toward sharing knowledge, to learn from other disciplines, to cooperate rather than compete.

> Many individual strands of knowledge and expertise relating to service systems already exist, but they often lie in unconnected silos. This no longer reflects the reality of interconnected economic activities which, for example, sees manufacturers of engineering products adopting service-oriented business models and health care providers learning lessons from modern manufacturing operations. Indeed, there are wide gaps in our knowledge and skills across silos.
>
> IfM and IBM (2008)

## WHO CAN BENEFIT FROM SERVICE SCIENCE?

The short answer to this question is—everyone.

Service Science has the potential to benefit individuals, businesses, nonprofits, governments, and society. Services need to be studied, analyzed, researched, improved, and brought to a state of the art in the way that manufacturing of products has been. Think of the industrial advances, for example in assembly line procedures, or in areas where the focus has been to gain the most profit in the least amount of time with the least amount of effort and still maintain a high quality product. Services, in turn, need to be more efficient and productive. One way to achieve this is to develop a discipline that uses science, technology, and business expertise to improve the quality and productivity of services.

Though at first glance this looks like a goal to simply make more profit for business, the service sector can be found in government, education, and health—areas in our lives that very much need to improve and expand their services for the public good. "We have no choice but to make services more science- and technology-based if we are to improve the value delivered from the services sector. This is true of not just IT services, but especially of other services such as health, education and government," says Robert Morris, vice president for services research at IBM Research (IBM, 2010).

Individuals and organizations dependent on complex service systems are all stakeholders of Service Science in that they need the knowledge and skills required for service innovation and service delivery. Individuals and families seek better education, better health care, better financial planning. Environmental and sustainability issues affect everyone.

Business and industry of course want to improve their profit margins and therefore have a clear interest in Service Science. Business maintains that we need to learn how to invest in service systems in order to improve key performance indicators, develop new services, improve existing service systems, and be masters of innovation. Firms seek to improve service quality and customer experience by creating new ideas and materials and new ways of delivering them.

Organizations in nonprofit sectors need Service Science as they seek to deliver their unique service offerings and remain financially viable. They are also under pressure to improve their productivity. Educational institutions that seek to develop an interdisciplinary and intercultural approach to service research are also beneficiaries. We can see an extended role for education in the twenty-first century as universities prepare people to be adaptive innovators. Governments, at both national and local levels, need a highly skilled workforce and infrastructures to improve their public service systems. They need to provide better services and communication with the public at every level.

Knowledge workers across a wide range of disciplines can also benefit. The past 20 years have seen the establishment of disciplines such as service marketing, service operations, service management, service engineering, service design, service computing, and many others. This knowledge can be applied in all disciplines dealing with services.

## FORWARD INTO SATISFACTION

Establishing a new science is no easy task, the challenges are many, starting with the existing structure of academia, the lack of resources for research of multidisciplinary topics, the inertia of (some) governments and organizations. The nay-sayers are many—called "contrarians" in some of the blogs. But the people who are the movers and shakers in this field are promoting it with a zeal that is a wonder to behold. A critical mass has been reached, and the momentum is carrying this new and vital addition to the world's knowledge base.

Thomas Kuhn (1962) tells us that science does not progress by simply adding new data to existing theories. Instead, when new evidence arises, and is proven true, science discards the old theory and reconstructs its theory to be consistent with the new evidence. Kuhn coined the term paradigm shift, and warned that these shifts cannot happen without a great deal of resistance. He describes the phases that occur when new ideas contradict an existing theory. First there is disdain and scorn. This is followed by doubt as to the new theory's validity. At the end, when the old theory can no longer be defended and is obviously out of date, the paradigm shifts into acceptance of the new evidence.

What is needed is not only collaboration across academic disciplines but also the doubling of R&D investment in service education and research by governments and business. Governments especially need to push forward their policies and invest in Service Science education and research. Business, academia, and government can do this together.

Should we keep saying that Service Science is nascent—that it is in the process of becoming? Service Science has come a long way from its early beginnings a decade ago. The impetus to continue to develop it is obvious. The will to allow it to be truly transdisciplinary will come from the forward thinkers in the separate departments and disciplines that comprise it. Perhaps we should stop calling it an emerging science. It seems that it is born, has learned to walk, and is learning many languages as its literature expands worldwide.

There is no looking back—the jump has been made no matter in what form it continues to grow, or in which home it will land. Service Science is moving forward, because, like the world in which we live, that is its nature.

We have examined the wave of the knowledge economy in which we live, following on the agricultural and industrial periods. We have seen that services have become the new "product" and that the economy is dynamically geared to new services and service innovation. We have looked at the obvious fact that a science of service is necessary and timely. We have discussed the invention of Service Science and the elements that have contributed to its growth. Next we will look at the synergies that exist between Service Science and the study of information.

I would like to end this chapter with the following quote from Pam Grout (2014), who writes about paradigm shifts:

> We live in a quantum age where people can instantaneously text each other across the planet, repair detached retinas with nothing but laser beams, and use little hand-held devices to get money-saving Groupons. Yet, in our thinking, in our application of these new truths, we're lagging sorely behind. We're still using industrial age thinking. We're not using the incredible power of our consciousness. Our consciousness which can, and does, create worlds.

# REFERENCES

Bell, D. (1973). *The coming of post-industrial society: A venture in social forecasting*. New York, NY: Basic Books.
Chesbrough, H., & Spohrer, J. (2006). A research manifesto for services science. *Communications of the ACM, 49*(7), 35–40.
Drucker, P. (1959). *Landmarks of tomorrow*. New York, NY: Harper & Brothers.
Drucker, P. (1994). The age of social transformation. *Atlantic Monthly, 274*(5), 53–80.
Finnish Employers Management Development Institute (FEMDI). (1991). Towards the 21st century, work in the 1990s. *International symposium on future trends in the changing working life*, 13–15 August 1991. Helsinki, Finland. *Proceedings 3*, Institute of Occupational Health, Helsinki.
Grout, P. (2014). *E-cubed*. Carlsbad, CA: Hay House.
Holstein W.J. (2006). And now a syllabus for the service economy. *New York Times*, 3 December. <http://www.webcitation.org/6acnAlmbv> Accessed April 2015.
IBM. (2010). IBM 100. Icons of progress series. *The invention of Service Science*. <http://www.webcitation.org/6acncnO8F> Accessed April 2015.
IfM & IBM (2008). *Succeeding through service innovation: A service perspective for education, research, business and government*. Cambridge, UK: University of Cambridge Institute for Manufacturing.
International Labour Organization. (2007). *Global Employment Trends Brief, January 2007*.
International Monetary fund. (2011). International Monetary Fund, World Economic Outlook Database: Nominal GDP list of countries. Data for the year 2010. Accessed April 2015.
Kuhn, T. (1962). *The structure of scientific revolutions*. Chicago, IL: University of Chicago Press.
Lovelock, C., Wirtz, J., & Chew, P. (2009). *Essentials of services marketing*. New York, NY: Prentice-Hall.
Maglio, P. P., Kieliszewski, C. A., & Spohrer, J. C. (Eds.), (2010). *Handbook of Service Science* New York, NY: Springer.
Maglio, P. P., & Spohrer, J. (2008). Fundamentals of Service Science. *Journal of the Academy of Marketing Science, 36*, 18–20.
Ostrom, A. L., Bitner, M. J., Brown, S. W., Burkhard, K. A., Goul, M., Smith-Daniels, V., et al. (2010). Moving forward and making a difference: research priorities for the science of service. *Journal of Service Research, 13*, 4. Originally published online 18 January 2010. <http://dx.doi.org/10.1177/1094670509357611>, <http://www.webcitation.org/6aco4aGnf> Accessed April 2015
Prusak, L. (2001). <http://www.webcitation.org/6acoAs0cP> Accessed April 2015.
Prusak, L., & Davenport, T. (1998). *Working knowledge: How organizations manage what they know*. Boston, MA: Harvard Business School Press.
Reich, R. (1992). *The work of nations: Preparing ourselves for 21st century capitalism*. New York, NY: Vintage Press.
Rust, R. T., & Huang, M.-H. (Eds.), (2014). *"Marketing: A Service Science and arts perspective,"* in *Handbook of service marketing research* Northampton, MA: Edward Elgar Publishing.
Spohrer, J. (2009). Editorial column – welcome to our declaration of interdependence. *Service Science, 1*(1), i–ii. <http://dx.doi.org/10.1287/serv.1.1.i> (Quote under Chapter 2 heading). Accessed April 2015.
Spohrer, J. (2011). <http://www.webcitation.org/6acoH2CUg> Accessed April 2015.
Spohrer, J., Fodell, D., & Murphy, W. (2012). 10 reasons why Service Science matters to universities. *EDUCAUSE Review, 47*(6), (November/December).
Vandermerwe, S., & Rada, J. (1988). Servitization of business: adding value by adding services. *European Management Journal, 6*(4), Winter.

# CHAPTER 3

# Synergies: Service Science and the Information Sector

> *Information is the world's next natural resource.*
> **Ginni Rometty, Chairman, President and Chief Executive Officer, IBM**

## PARTICIPATING IN THE SERVICE SCIENCE EXPLOSION

People, information, technology, organization: does this sound familiar? Is this Service Science or Information Science, or both? An argument can be made for the makings of a good marriage of similar as well as complementary elements in both disciplines. The similarities of the goals of the two disciplines are many, as we shall see.

Who is doing the research, teaching the subject, and receiving the grants?

They are the faculties and schools of Computer Science, Management, Engineering, and Business and Administration. So we are in good company. Can a case can be made for schools of Information becoming proactive in this arena? Yes, a case can be made. If any profession today is dealing with people, technology, and information, it is the knowledge worker in information.

## INFORMATION PROFESSIONALS AND SERVICE

As information professionals, we have studied service, given service, trained in service, trained others in how to give service, measured service, and applied the concept of service in the front office, in the back office, and in the streets. Information, technology, and people are the elements that we study and work with on a daily basis in the service systems in which we work. Information technology is embedded in all aspects of our work. Our service expertise is based on knowledge and access to the content that technology offers. So what do we have to learn about a science of service?

First of all, it is important to know about exciting and challenging new directions and innovations in this vast arena called information. The information professional is situated front row center in the service economy. This is one of the reasons this book was written. The rapid growth of the service economy has had an impact on all aspects of our society and jobs are increasingly based on information and knowledge services. Demand is growing for workers with the knowledge and skills to be effective in this new economy.

Information professionals would agree that their work is in the service sector and that they strive to provide the services that they think their clients need. In fact, all information institutions are service systems. We need to know and explore the issues developing in our information-based economy. Because service is the major component of the information practices of the future, all systems will see significant shifts in their approach.

## THE ECONOMY AND SERVICE SCIENCE

What is our role in this economy? Our role has always been based in information! Now that the rest of the world has caught up, we need to see the new big picture and how we can play in it. A brand new vista of opportunity has opened up, with choices full of surprises and growth.

Information professionals are already applying some of the principles found in Service Science. We measure performance, we have methods of evaluating client satisfaction, we innovate in services, we market our centers and services, and we strive to increase the quality of our services. Service Science can help us do this in a more systematic, dare I say scientific, manner, giving us new methods and models for evaluation, for innovation, for understanding needs, and for studying the positive and negative impact of new services. It can show us how to combine formal models with models of human behavior to understand the efficacy of our services.

The vantage point of a multidisciplinary offer is a powerful place. Innovation often occurs when individuals or groups move to the connecting points between disciplines. Steve Jobs often spoke of his love for the intersection of the humanities and technology.

## THE ENERGY OF NEW VISTAS

Ideas from management, science, and engineering as applied to the understanding of service-driven organizations can intersect with knowledge work. Service Science calls for more systematic innovation. It asks the question, how is innovation encouraged and established? Can we can create and innovate with more systematic methods? Can we increase the scope of our offer to better distribute this knowledge? These questions and their answers are pursued in the study of Service Science.

There is a lot to be learned from Service Science concerning the needs and changing expectations of our public. We can capitalize on growth opportunities by looking at our services from other points of view. Service Science can show, for example, the time saved in information search and delivery, therefore the lowering of costs. Could we gain better knowledge of information mining? Can we better apply SOA (service-oriented architecture) and web services to implement service systems? The knowledge being articulated in Service Science can be used by our profession, and can lead to the development of new and better services.

Authors He and Wang (2008) argue for the fact that old methods of service can no longer meet the needs of users in information institutions. They describe the old notion that maintained that service could be improved by adding a digital component to traditional services such as reference services, for example. They argue that this type of cosmetic change is not enough from a Service Science point of view, which would concentrate more on people and pay more attention to creating value.

## RESEARCH OPPORTUNITIES

Information professionals have had and have now an important role in research. We provide an infrastructure for research—the information infrastructure—without which research cannot be done. And we need to be doing more original research ourselves.

Davenport and Prusak (1998), writing about knowledge brokers, say that librarians are suited by temperament and their capacity as knowledge guides to be experts in people-to-people as well as people-to-text connections. In the corporate world librarians are indispensable knowledge brokers. However,

> The merits of their activities are never measured or captured by human resource systems. . . . It is much harder to measure the profit they help generate than the

*cost to the company of their salaries and benefits.... They have no familiar ways to quantify the benefits of a library as an information source and knowledge marketplace.*
***Davenport and Prusak (1998)***

In the information sector, and most likely in many others, information professionals supply professionals in their organizations as well as consultants coming in with access to a tremendous wealth of material and connections with people doing similar work worldwide. They help their clients ask the right questions of the information they provide, and guide their research in order to save them precious time. It is becoming good practice that they receive credit in the publishing of the report, article, or book that is written as a consequence of their assistance. Acknowledgement of their work could become a prerequisite at the beginning of a project requiring their assistance.

Service Science involves partnerships with business and government and thus opens up sources of funding for the research, development, and teaching of this new discipline. Because Service Science is based on the relationship between people, technology, organizations, and information, this research yields models, methodologies, processes, and software tools that create and deliver services more efficiently. A better understanding of human behavior is also critical. The resources of social sciences such as psychology, sociology, and anthropology provide useful information about the way people and groups work and interact. We can benefit from behavioral observation studies and by learning how to measure perception, for instance.

## TWO MAJOR STUDIES FOR RESEARCH PRIORITIES IN SERVICES

The Centre for Services Leadership at the WP Carey School of Business at Arizona State University ran an amazing 18-month study to establish a set of global, interdisciplinary research priorities and to outline a foundation for the science of service (Ostrom et al., 2010). This remarkable effort included the participation of over 300 participants: academics from a variety of disciplines, business executives from a wide range of companies and geographies, and different levels of government leaders. The study led to the naming of 10 research priorities for this new discipline. Each priority includes a list of targeted research topics for business executives, academics, and government leaders. Each priority also contains several important and more specific topic areas for service research.

> *The intent is that the priorities will spur service research by shedding light on the areas of greatest value and potential return to academia, business, and government. Through academic, business, and government collaboration, we can enhance our understanding of service and create new knowledge to help tackle the most important opportunities and challenges we face today.*
>
> **Ostrom et al. (2010)**

This study served as a strong point of reference for academics, business, and government and gave a solid, practical roadmap for future research and policy decisions. This paper became one of the most cited in this area, is extremely readable for business, government, policy makers, interested public, and of course, academics and researchers.

Although this study was done in 2010, the relevance of all 10 priorities for information professionals remains intact. The examples given are important for information professionals, and cover a wide range of participants, including industry, business, government, as well as academics. Their comments are important and relevant, thus the decision to include the findings of this study We can contribute to these research goals, both as a system in which research can be done, as well as taking on the research ourselves in our service systems.

The research priorities given in this study are organized by three aspects of business: *strategy, development,* and *execution*. The following very selective summary describes the 10 priorities for research within these three sections, and importantly, their relevance to the information professions.

1. *Fostering service infusion and growth*

    This first research priority is an obvious one. In order to change from being goods-dominant to goods and services-dominant, organizations need new business models that result in growth and expansion based on services.

    Tom Esposito, CEO of The INSIGHT Group, and formerly Vice President of Global Consulting and Services, IBM, gives the following, very relevant points:

    > *Two seemingly small business strategy changes have had a significant impact in enabling the service culture to gain traction in product-driven firms. The first change was adding an s at the end of service. This small change to services helped firms create a vast array of innovative fee-based services offerings aimed at helping customers accelerate the adoption of their products and business solutions. The second change was adjusting the focus from service in support of products to services in support of customers.. ... Sustainable success experienced by firms such as IBM and General Electric can be attributed to the*

*recognition that product and services businesses each need to be managed by different business models.*

Esposito's two seemingly simple points—adding an s at the end of service, (amazing and astute), and changing the focus of services in support of products, to services in support of customers—have created a great deal of leverage in the subject of Service Science.

Information professionals have been innovative in the last decades in terms of moving from providing depositories to teaching the public how to be information pro's, and providing community services that no one else was giving, such as being lifelong learning partners to clients from the ages of 1–100. Services have undergone not only a shift in the types and numbers of services provided, but even more importantly in attitudes and personality profiles in the profession.

2. *Improving well-being through transformative service*

Transformative service research (TSR) is defined as "service research that centers on creating uplifting changes and improvements in the well-being of both individuals and communities." TSR seeks to better the quality of life of present and future generations of consumers and citizens through services. Several specific topics were brought forward within the framework of this study, including improving consumer and societal welfare through service; enhancing access, quality, and productivity in health care and education; and delivering service in a sustainable manner, one that preserves health, society, and the environment.

This area created the most excitement and enthusiasm from the participants in the study, and we can certainly understand why. It reads like a manual on how to make a better world.

One of the people doing the commentaries for this report, Michael Lyons, Chief Researcher, Service and Systems Science, British Telecom Innovation and Design, put it this way:

*Sustainable development requires a holistic approach because actions to improve one issue can lead to increased pressures elsewhere. The emerging information and communication technologies (ICT)-based knowledge economy may form part of the solution but only if technological developments are accompanied by complementary changes in socioeconomic behaviour.*

This includes relationship development, social interaction, and the impact of the customer's role in consumption and value creation.

There are brilliant commentaries on all seven topics in TSR. Although we can't include them all here, this section of the study is totally relevant for information professionals, and definitely recommended reading.

The commentaries include opinions on improving consumer and societal welfare, the need for research in enhancing health care, the need for research in delivering service in a sustainable manner, and key research questions related to service infrastructure and public services.

3. *Creating and maintaining a service culture*

The challenge here is how to develop and sustain a service culture, a service mind-set, as well as creating a learning service organization in a product-based company or institution. Globalizing a service organization's culture across different countries is also an important element.

We begin to see that a service culture is not only the services we offer outside the organization, it is also the culture inside—learning, teaching, developing, and recruiting service-oriented teams.

A government example of creating a service culture comes from the state of Georgia in the United States, which launched a Customer Service Initiative in 2005. The goal was to develop an enterprise-wide culture of service after studying their agencies, employees, services, and customers. Joe Doyle, Administrator of the Governor's Office of Consumer Affairs in the State of Georgia, states:

*Our work [the Customer Service Initiative] provides one model for improvement of customer service in government. I would welcome the validation of our research by other public sector entities. In addition, our work leads to several important macro-level issues worthy of additional study. These include the following:*
- *Why do taxpayers (i.e., "customers" of government services) tolerate the current level of service provided?*
- *What is the tipping point for government organizations to realize that both a new standard and a higher bar need to be set on service?*
- *What will it take for government organizations to transition from being the "employer of last resort" to the "employer of choice"?*

This initiative provides an apt model for any level of government taking on services research in order to develop a service culture. Bravo to a government department that can ask itself these tough questions and be ready to listen to customers and to change its culture. We have all been privy to situations in a public service where a member of the personnel can make or break a transaction that we really need, sometimes waiting in line for an hour or two or three and being told no, emphatically and irremediably. No business would survive with this type of "customer service," yet we put up with it in publicly funded departments that do not give us the service we want or deserve. We hope that this government example can serve as a precedent for others to follow.

4. *Stimulating service innovation*

Haluk Demirkan, PhD, summarizes the discussion on service innovation in the following way:

*Research is needed on how to innovate customer-centric service, on how companies are identifying hidden customer needs and how to transform them into radical innovations. Both industry and academia need to develop state-of-the-art customer-centric service innovation processes and ensure their implementation by researchers across different disciplines. Finally, government policy makers need to promote and support service innovation as part of their economic development strategies because of the growing contribution of services to national and regional economies.*

New concepts, new approaches, and new techniques—this is the message for innovation for the information sector—it's already happening, we just need more of it.

5. *Enhancing service design*

The literature shows an abundance of best practices and case studies of companies that have succeeded in doing service design. What is perhaps missing is how these companies deal with innovation and design that is future-oriented.

A different take on service design can be seen from the point of view of the arts, and designing services that respond to emotional needs. Raymond Fisk, Professor and Chair at the Marketing Department of Texas State University—San Marcos, in his commentary writes about the arts as being ancient forms of emotional design:

*Thus, the arts have much to contribute to cross-disciplinary service design. For example, great theatrical performances provoke laughter or sadness on cue. Few service organizations are skilled at designing experiences to provoke emotions in this way. Investigation into the cocreation of emotional content in service experiences, drawing on the arts as foundational disciplines, could be very valuable*

This is a challenge for service design for the future, and promises a very exciting development to which we can look forward.

6. *Optimizing service networks and value chains*

As in most business and government endeavors, the service network can lead to profitable collaboration. Two important research areas targeted as crucial for the evolution of service networks and value chains are (1) developing service network collaboration between organizations and (2) creating distributed service networks on a global scale.

A good example of optimizing service networks is given by Elliot Rabinovich, Associate Professor of Supply Chain Management at Arizona State University. He suggests that the sharing of information among networks of service providers in the health care industry, for example, can improve the speed and accuracy in the diagnosis and treatment of illnesses as well as avoiding replicating the same functionalities in the network.

Researchers could try to understand how to better distribute service networks globally. In terms of information sharing, Paul Maglio, Senior Manager, Service Systems Research at the IBM Almaden Research Center, sums up its raison d'être in two sentences:

*"The biggest research opportunity lies not in technology for information sharing, but rather in the larger context of human communication. That is what information sharing is for."*

That says it all.

Information professionals have been sharing resources even before interlibrary loan, creating consortiums to leverage buying power with publishers, and acting as early adopters of new technologies that are then shared with their clients and colleagues in the information professions.

7. *Effectively branding and selling services*

We know a great deal about the branding of goods and products, but little about branding services that are intangible and experiential in nature. However, many examples of services with strong branding exist. Among the oldest ones, the Mayo Clinic has had a reliable reputation for health care for over a century, relying on word-of-mouth rather than any advertising of any kind. More recent examples include Google, Yahoo, Starbucks, PayPal, Amazon, Netflix, among others. A good question is evoked: How have the leading service brands been able to connect/engage with buyers at the sensory, cognitive, emotional, behavioral, and social levels? Also, with the advent of both social media and consumer reviews on the Web, how does a service business ensure that the customer experience is not only rated at the top, but is strong enough to go viral?

> As more companies embark on the profitable but difficult migration from products to services, service branding and its double impact on external and internal customers will become an issue that companies and researchers should address.
>
> **Luciano Arosemena**
> **Service Sales Manager Abbott Laboratories, Colombia**

In fact, some information specialists are successfully branding their services, but this is an area that needs further research as well as compilations of best practices.

8. *Enhancing the service experience through co-creation*

Co-creation here means that the entity offering the service and the entity receiving the service each has a role to play in the service experience. Stephen L. Vargo, PhD Professor of Marketing at the University of Hawai'i at Manoa is a thought leader in services and service dominant logic. He says that value is being reconceptualized as co-created by firms *and* customers, each in the context of their own networks of resource access.

There is everything to be done in this area. Though all the research priorities stated in this section are important, there is one commentary that is particularly relevant to information professionals. It concerns co-creating services with customers as an active participant, not as a passive consumer. Customers are a good, if not the best, source of ideas from what they want from a service. We should shift from thinking we are the sole experts and invite clients to be active partners in what we are offering. On the other hand, however, Steve Jobs was a great proponent of inventing products and their services *before* the customer knew they wanted and absolutely needed it.

Further, according to Anders Gustafsson, PhD, Professor, Service Research Center (CTF), Karlstad University, Sweden, methods of working with customers such as focus groups, surveys, and interviews are a backward look at what has already happened, whereas what is needed are forward-looking techniques that bring about an active understanding of service experiences.

9. *Measuring and optimizing the value of service*

Services are much more difficult to measure than products. What is needed is to identify, implement, track, and find the value of the service in the customer experience. This process is still in its infancy and provides an open area for needed research.

Chris Melocik, Senior Vice President, Integration and Process Improvement, Republic Services, Inc., describes the need for measuring services in this way:

*Organizations struggle to justify investments to deliver improved or additional services. Intuitively, these investments are consistent with customer desires and appear to be the right actions for strategic success. However, without a means to predict the value of the investment and then to measure actual versus expected impact, service initiatives are continually deprioritized. These initiatives cannot survive the competition for capital and resources in strategic and annual planning processes*

There is a need for developing the right metrics to measure non-monetary costs such as the loss of customers because of poorly designed services, or the cost benefits of customer loyalty. In other words, finding methodologies to quantify the value of service, a non-material entity.

The information professional knows only too well the challenge of convincing their hierarchies of the value of their invisible services. Going forward with the right metrics would be helpful indeed.

10. *Leveraging technology to advance service: this encompasses the other nine priorities*

Finally, the role of technology, which pervades all nine research priorities, is counted as the tenth priority. The terms service and technology conjure a broad spectrum of unique viewpoints.

Michael Goul from Arizona State University describes the term "freedom economy" as one that scholars have adopted to describe the context in which customers are at the center of boundaryless relationships and low-friction transactions, exchanges, and business operations. There has been a subtle paradigm shift—the freedom economy capabilities come to the customer rather than the other way around, and customers in the freedom economy expect new choices and will define value wherever, whenever, and however they want.

Smart devices and the Internet of Things (discussed in Chapter 4) will change the way companies create and sustain value for their customers.

R. Gary Bridge, PhD, Senior Vice President, Internet Business Solutions Group, Cisco Systems, states that:

*Services productivity has lagged behind manufacturing productivity, but is poised for breakthrough gains through digitized content, more mobility, and cloud computing, all of which enable new services*

Information professionals know that their offer has evolved and has provided services not dreamt of even a few years ago. Keeping up with this research is of great importance to us, not only from a general current-culture point of view, but also to innovate services in this sector that result from yet another leap ahead in technology.

## FAST FORWARD TO 2015

Just before the final manuscript for this book was submitted, a new study was shared with me by MaryJo Bitner, Service Research Priorities in a Rapidly Changing Context (Ostrom, Parasuraman, Bowen, Patricio, & Voss, 2015). In fact, the 2010 study serves as a basis, if not a prerequisite for the appreciation of the 2015 study. The 2015 study covers the academic disciplines that are involved with services and is practical in showing what research is actually being done and will continue to be done. It is, in part, an iteration of the research priorities given in 2010 and what has occurred in the interim.

The 2015 study is as impressive as the first one in terms of design and scope. It is more precise as a result of the 5 years that have gone by, giving the researchers the opportunity to survey a great number of academics who were involved in services work. Some of the survey results were surprising, and this study gives us a closer, more practical look at the services research that has already been done, is being done, and will be done in the future.

The 2010 study had 10 research priorities, discussed earlier. The 2015 study has 12. Here they are:
1. Stimulating service innovation.
2. Facilitating servitization, service infusion, and solutions.
3. Understanding organization and employee issues relevant to successful service.
4. Developing service networks and systems.
5. Leveraging service design.
6. Using big data to advance service.

7. Understanding value creation.
8. Enhancing the service experience.
9. Improving well-being through transformative service.
10. Measuring and optimizing service performance and impact.
11. Understanding service in a global context.
12. Leveraging technology to advance service.

There are two new additions to the priorities listed in 2010: using big data to advance service, and understanding service in a global context.

In the authors' words,

> Given the significant changes and growing research interest in the service domain since the previous research-priority-setting work by Ostrom et al. (2010), it is useful to develop a new iteration of priorities that leverages both global and diverse discipline input. It is also worthwhile to uncover critical research-related issues currently facing the service field and to explore ways of addressing them to advance the field.

> A substantial change from 2010 was the compelling case for including big data as a priority in 2015, given the focus on how data can be used to design and enhance service ... Furthermore, this 2015 iteration witnessed something of a "global" revolution, with increased mention of the global aspects of service and much global flavor in the qualitative data, leading to its addition as a cross-cutting priority.
>
> **Ostrom et al. (2015)**

The study involved academics in a variety of disciplines throughout the world, though it reflects more responses to the online survey from marketing academics than from other disciplines.

The importance of research for our profession cannot be overemphasized, and these two studies are significant guideposts in keeping up with research that is being done in services, as well as launching research work in information.

## A NEW PROFILE FOR THE KNOWLEDGE WORKER

A new profile for the skills and abilities of knowledge workers for the twenty-first century has made its appearance. As information professionals need to develop and explore future roles in the information economy, an important part of our redefinition can result from our participation in Service Science.

These knowledge workers are called T-shaped professionals. These professionals have a deep knowledge of one or two areas of study (the vertical bar of the T) and the expertise and communication skills to be able to collaborate across many disciplines and to apply knowledge in areas other than their own (the horizontal bar of the T). This new profile is big news, and it bears signaling to all faculties and schools as a necessity for any professional in the knowledge economy. As the service sector grows, T-shaped skills built by disciplines like Service Science will be in growing demand.

Companies such as McKinsey, Apple, IBM, and Procter and Gamble hire T-shaped people, though they don't necessarily call them that.

Tim Brown, CEO of IDEO, a leading design firm that is ranked as one of the most innovative in the world, says that he hires only T-shaped people.

> *T-shaped people have two kinds of characteristics, hence the use of the letter "T" to describe them. The vertical stroke of the "T" is a depth of skill that allows them to contribute to the creative process. That can be from any number of different fields: an industrial designer, an architect, a social scientist, a business specialist or a mechanical engineer. The horizontal stroke of the "T" is the disposition for collaboration across disciplines. It is composed of two things. First, empathy. It's important because it allows people to imagine the problem from another perspective—to stand in somebody else's shoes. Second, they tend to get very enthusiastic about other people's disciplines, to the point that they may actually start to practise them. T-shaped people have both depth and breadth in their skills.*
>
> Hansen (2010) Reprinted with permission, Chief Executive magazine/Chief Executive Group, (c) 2010.

The digital age requires this type of employee. In-depth skill in one discipline is no longer enough. Creativity, ability to collaborate and communicate have come into importance in balancing out the requirements for success in recruitment.

TANK, an Australian brand agency with clients such as Holden, Australia Post, and Virgin, exclusively hires T-shaped staff because they are most effective at generating and executing new ideas.

> *We need people who can generate ideas, who can think laterally and creatively and can cross-pollinate across disciplines. The need to have a broad range of experiences and a linear depth of expertise is crucial*
>
> Birchall (2012)

Dr. Phil Gardner, at Michigan State University, describes the ideal job candidate as a "liberal arts student with technical skills" or a "business/

engineering student with humanities training"—in other words, a T-shaped candidate. He notes that "while the engineers are out in front on this concept—every field will require T professional development" (Brooks, 2012).

The Institute for the Future (IFTF), based in Palo Alto California, has been a leader in foresight methodologies, such as the Delphi technique, a method of aggregating expert opinions to develop plausible predictions in various areas. They called on experts in many fields in order to prehend what would be the *Ten Skills for the Future Workforce*. In addition to T-shaped skills like sense making, social intelligence, novel and adaptive thinking, we find transdisciplinarity, which is literacy in and an ability to understand concepts across multiple disciplines. The report states that

> While throughout the 20th century, ever-greater specialization was encouraged, the next century will see transdisciplinary approaches take center stage. We are already seeing this in the emergence of new areas of study, such as nanotechnology, which blends molecular biology, biochemistry, protein chemistry, and other specialties... The ideal worker of the next decade is "T-shaped"—they bring deep understanding of at least one field, but have the capacity to converse in the language of a broader range of disciplines. This requires a sense of curiosity and a willingness to go on learning far beyond the years of formal education. As extended lifespans promote multiple careers and exposure to more industries and disciplines, it will be particularly important for workers to develop this T-shaped quality
>
> **Institute for the Future (2011)**

Bell and Shank (2007) point out that T-shaped library staff possess principle skill, that is, a body of traditional competences (the vertical leg of the T), but they are so sensitive to their users' broader educational needs, they cultivate other skills (the top horizontal leg of the T) and do them as well, to varying degrees that is. In other words, T-shaped people are inquisitive and try to integrate the skills of what others do in their own work.

It would appear that information professionals in many sectors consider themselves to be T-shaped professionals, having advanced degrees in subject specialties to which they add a post-graduate degree in information studies, which includes practice and expertise in communication skills, psychology, and other areas in the social sciences.

## AN ACADEMIC HOME FOR SERVICE SCIENCE

Information institutions *are* service systems, and represent a goldmine for research in Service Science. This domain is in constant evolution, always reinventing itself and its services. Most of the research in Service Science is being done in the corporate sector. There is no doubt that more research is needed in the public sector, although there is an awakening to this need in some countries.

Service Science needs an academic home—it touches on many disciplines including Computer Science, Systems Engineering, Cognitive Science, Economics, Organizational Behavior, Human Resources Management, Marketing, Operations Research, and others. Some Service Science programs are being taught in various departments and schools, but its multidisciplinary requirements are not necessarily being met in the vertically designed silos of knowledge. Dr. Kelly Lyons, a professor in the iSchool at the University of Toronto, put forth a proposal: that Service Science find its academic home in iSchools (Lyons, 2010).

At this point we will take a brief look at this phenomenon called iSchools before continuing with this proposal.

## iSCHOOLS

There have been changes in focus and in name of schools of information studies in the decades that led to the emergence of information schools, or iSchools. The iSchool movement began in the 1990s and was formally named in 2005 by a collective of Information Schools "dedicated to advancing the information field in the 21st century" (http://www.webcitation.org/6ah8t0iVg).

Presently there are 65 iSchools worldwide, and the number is growing. The majority are in the United States, the rest being in Europe, China, Australia, South Korea, Singapore, Japan, and Canada. Not many of these schools actually have the name iSchool in their name or on their website. Some state that they are members of the iSchool; for example, the University of Boras, in Sweden.

In 2014 the iSchools became a legal corporation under the laws of the District of Columbia in the United States. This is a significant step toward establishing the iSchools as a permanent entity. Perhaps this will lead to schools proudly displaying their iSchool status in a visible manner in the near future.

The core vision of the iSchool is the study of the interaction of information, technology, and people, all three elements having equal importance. By definition this means a multiple approach:

*The study of information is interdisciplinary, fed by multiple diverse fields. Librarianship and computer science have historically been the primary feeders of the field, but information studies is also fed by fields such as education, psychology, anthropology, business, journalism—indeed, the range of social sciences*

*http://www.webcitation.org/6ah8t0iVg*

*The perfect merger of academic rigor and contemporary thinking has come together in the concept of iSchools, which give practical consideration and interesting learning opportunities to the most relevant issue of our time: information.*

*Swan (2014)*

Schools of Computer Science joined the movement, as did Schools of Information Systems, Schools of Information Management, and of course Schools of Library and Information Science, Schools of Information, and Schools of Information Studies. Some of the iSchools give more emphasis to education, for example, UCLA; some to communication, for example, Rutgers. This academic convergence already gives the strong signal that a multidisciplinary vision is being shared, coming from diverse origins in many high-profile universities.

*While each individual iSchool has its own strengths and specializations, together they share a fundamental interest in the relationships between information, people, and technology*

*http://www.ischools.org*

It appears that graduates of iSchools are doing well in the job market, including in academics, nonprofits, government, and industry, and that iSchool faculty is doing important and respected research. iProfessionals listed on the website include categories such as usability engineers, information architects, network managers, project managers, web developers, business/systems analysts, web designers, software development engineers, information assurance professionals, IT analysts and managers, e-Learning program managers, applications managers, programmers, competitive intelligence analysts, and knowledge management specialists. These and other appellations that are included in the domain of information professionals are obviously enlarging the scope and multidisciplinarity of this area.

Is this movement sustainable? Olson and Grudin (2009), are generally optimisic for the future of iSchools, as they consider that the study of information has only just begun.

I asked them whether, 3 years later, they were still enthusiastic and optimistic about iSchools. In an e-mail exchange, Gary Olson said,

*Yes, we are still enthusiastic about the idea.*

Co-author Jonathan Grudin said,

*I'm optimistic, but this is against a backdrop of challenges to institutions of higher education that instill some uncertainty about the nature of scholarly disciplines in the future. Still, I would think that information is one that will thrive if any do*

Robert Glushko, professor at the iSchool at the University of California Berkeley, describes the iSchool like this:

*…the academic unit in which I teach service system design is a School of Information (or "iSchool"), a novel kind of university program that might be described as either "the intersection of business, computer science, and social science" or "a 21st century library school". Either characterization suggests a focus on the design of information intensive systems and services (Apte & Mason, 1995) with a strong emphasis on technology and its organizational or social context. Neither characterization does justice to the aggressive way that most iSchools are developing a multi or transdisciplinary character as they seek to prepare students for a society and economy that is increasingly information driven and services led.*

*Glushko (2011)*

An excellent study on the research interests of iSchool faculty was done by Holmberg, Tsou, and Sugimoto (2013). They give a very thorough and fascinating description of the genesis of iSchools and their evolution. Specifically, research questions this study asks are, what is the current research landscape of the iSchools? And what types of shared research interests are there among the iSchools? This study is a must read for information professionals interested in or involved in research. Another study on the state of academic research was done by Wu, He, Jiang, Dong, and Vo (2012).

Although some of the research being done is still based on information topics, there is a steady move toward a multidisciplinary approach to research in iSchools. This is applauded and encouraged.

## THE iSCHOOL PROPOSAL

Going back to Dr. Lyons' proposal, she and her team did a review of iSchool universities to identify which faculties, schools, or departments are pursuing courses, programs, and research in Service Science. Of the

23 universities that had iSchools, 12 had some Service Science programs, courses, or activities through their business schools or marketing faculties. Eight had SSME content in Engineering or Computer Science faculties, and five had a Service Science presence in their iSchool. These iSchools were at the University of California Berkeley, University of Michigan, Pennsylvania State University, Singapore Management University, and the University of Toronto. Of these five, only three iSchools were actually teaching Service Science: the University of California Berkeley, Singapore Management University, and the University of Toronto.

Lyons presents strong arguments that iSchools are an ideal place to engage in Service Science research and teaching because their vision involves a transdisciplinary participation and requires input from science, business, education, and culture.

A presentation by Lyons to the ISSIP in 2013 (http://www.webcitation.org/6ah9YvjeY) on the same topic showed a slight change in the numbers—six iSchools had included Service Science as opposed to five, and 11 universities with iSchools taught Service Science through their Engineering and Computer Science faculties rather than 12. Would a look at the present-day curricula of iSchools show a significant change in the number of schools teaching Service Science? The number of iSchools has increased substantially since 2010, and we would certainly hope that a good number of them have included this important emerging science for their students in this knowledge economy! A review and update of this important study is certainly called for.

Lyons' premises show a number of parallels between the requirements of Service Science and the mission and vision of iSchools, therefore it merits inclusion here. As we have seen, service systems are made up of people, information, organizations, and technology. iSchools are interested in the relationship between information, people, and technology. Both Service Science and iSchools recognize the importance of engaging the participation of partners in industry, academia, and government. Both Service Science and iSchools require a multidisciplinary approach. Lyons maintains that "... multidisciplinary hurdles are not only being overcome in iSchools, but being exploited to enhance the research and education of information professionals". It is true that the literature speaks of the difficulties and hardships of communicating across disciplines and the complications those multidisciplinary studies engender (Glushko, 2008). Nevertheless, it appears that the younger iSchool faculty members have worked out languages and cultures to bridge boundaries between their specialized fields, while keeping their common focus on information.

Lyons concludes:

*Not only will the iSchools be able to branch into and help define an important emerging discipline... and have access to industry partnerships and funding in the area, but Service Science will benefit tremendously from the iSchools multi-disciplinary approach to research and knowledge about the connections among information, technology and people*

Is Lyons's proposal reasonable? Yes, I believe it is. There is no other discipline that can provide a transdisciplinary environment with the same elements—a key requirement for this new science. New ideas, innovation, and growth can energize both disciplines across the board. Service Science will benefit from a transdisciplinary movement with a wealth of knowledge on the relationship between people, information, and technology. The synergy between the two can be energetically exploited by both sides.

## WHO IS TEACHING WHAT?

With a little help from our friends at IBM, programs and courses in Service Science began to be taught in various institutions around the world, mainly in graduate Business, Engineering, and Computer Science schools. Some offered formal SSME degree programs, others integrated Service Science across various disciplines. Many other schools created cross-disciplinary programs, including Carnegie Mellon, University of Michigan, and the University of Pennsylvania, combining courses in the Business, Engineering and Computer/Information Science schools.

Today more than 450 universities offer a Service Science program—a mix of computer science, social science, and business management. Schools in various parts of the world with interdisciplinary interests in Service Science include the University of Manchester, Helsinki University of Technology, University of Sydney, Karlsruhe Institute of Technology, Wuhan University China, National University of Singapore, Singapore Management University, Masaryk University, Lusofona University Information Systems School (Portugal), Aalto University in Finland, National Cheng Chi University in Taiwan, University of Toronto, the University of Applied Sciences Western Switzerland, and the University of Twente in the Netherlands, to name a few.

Switzerland, well reputed for its expertise in services, has a unique approach to the topic, leaning more toward the importance and value of the human interaction element than on the strictly algorithmic approach. Dr. Emmanuel Fragnière of the Geneva School of Business Administration speaks of the social codes and systems of belief that drive the service experience. Through a process of ethnomethodology (Fragnière & Sitten, 2012) he teaches that the invisible attributes of service can be made tangible.

In his Service Lab, through scriptwriting and role plays, he teaches how to redesign, safeguard (risk management), price, and test new services. Hundreds of students have been introduced to the process of ethnomethodology and have designed their own services.

First, students go to the service providers and service consumers and observe the everyday scenarios that take place in the service environment, noting the path of both the service provider and the client. They also conduct semi-directed interviews with the service providers, staff, and clients. Once this information is processed, they develop a script, which makes visible or "tangibilizes" the main service attributes of the experience. These attributes enable them to design a script that uncovers the covert, unidentified aspects of a service scenario. Theatre directors, actors, students, and participants from the stakeholder groups re-enact the scenario using the script. Everyone can review the service interaction as it is replayed. Qualitative analysis is performed and discussed and survey research can be done during and after each role play. The main role of the Service Lab is to train students in the practice of Service Science, and to examine the service design methodology in a variety of contexts.

It has also enabled students to become designers for service companies. Service designers are very important for the economy, especially in Switzerland. Fragnière believes that innovation in services is more of a sociological than a technological phenomenon, emerging from the streets rather than from the R&D departments. Taking the example of hotel management, a Swiss, César Ritz (1850—1918) was one of the great service designers. He created luxury hotels and added innovations that were totally new at the time: a bathroom in each room, planned events and outings for his rich customers, décor that added to the ambiance, a personalized rapport with each, and so on. Ritz had not succeeded in school nor in his apprenticeship as a waiter. But he liked people and people liked him. He knew how to design services that people loved, and that gave him a renowned name in the world of hotel design and management. The term "ritzy" is still used today.

Fragnière is of the opinion that the industrial models for designing services, which emphasize cost control, rapid execution, and standardization, are outmoded and no longer relevant.

> In today's growing service economy, it is essential for service providers in both the public and private sectors to understand the important roles that creativity, empathy and implicit knowledge play in service co-production in order to meet the demand for highly customized, expertise-dependent service experiences.
>
> *Fragnière and Sitten (2011)*

One of the top best practices of teaching Service Science, one that makes sense, takes the human element into consideration, communicates the bottom line logic of why we need to study Service Science, and does so in a transdisciplinary, practical and interesting way is being taught by Dr. Paul Maglio, one of the founders of Service Science.

Paul Maglio is Professor of Technology Management at the University of California, Merced, and a research staff member at IBM Research, Almaden. He is one of the founders of the field of Service Science. He is the Editor-in-Chief of Service Science, serves on the editorial board of the *Journal of Service Research*, and was lead editor of the *Handbook of Service Science*. He has published more than 100 papers in Computer Science, Cognitive Science, and Service Science.

He was immediately helpful and generous when I asked him whether I could describe how he teaches Service Science in this book. He has been teaching Service Science since 2007 and his syllabi show a consistently excellent and evolving approach to sharing his knowledge of Service Science.

His course description of Service Science at University of California Merced (Maglio, 2014) describes its importance in the following way:

> In this course, you will learn about service. You will learn what service is, why it is different from other sectors and other jobs, and why it is important. You will learn about problems in service, such as measuring performance, increasing quality, and creating innovation. You will learn how some have recently begun to study service from a variety of different perspectives—including social sciences, cognitive science, management, engineering, and others—to address these problems. This new approach is called Service Science. You will learn how this kind of interdisciplinary research might be effective in studying and understanding service. In the end, you will be able to have an informed and intelligent conversation about the nature of service, how to think about measurement in service, and how to increase innovation in service. And you will be (at least a little more) ready for the workforce you are about to enter.

Maglio's detailed syllabus (http://www.webcitation.org/6ah9nlAPR) can serve as a complete and very useful guide for professors who are or will be teaching Service Science. Students can approach this topic from a transdisciplinary stance, and it begins with the basics. He has provided us with a clear map of how to teach this wonderful subject.

An excellent avenue for the study of the science of services is the W. P. Carey School of Business at Arizona State University, which offers the W. P. Carey MBA Specialization in Strategic Marketing and Services Leadership.

*With a solid foundation in objective, scientific methods and proven marketing strategy, students learn the science behind service and receive a unique set of skills that are aggressively sought across all industries*

The Center for Services Leadership is a groundbreaking research center within the W. P. Carey School of Business. Here science from the academic world meets business strategy in an ultimately practical manner and prepares the millennials for the type of workforce they are about to enter.

The CSL was created in 1985 and pioneered the study of service while others were still focusing on products and manufacturing. Today, the Center is a "globally recognized authority and thought leader in the science of competing strategically through the profitable use of services."

Research at CSL is problem-focussed, working with companies and industry who are interested in developing a competitive edge through services. They offer executive and professional development programs.

The Centre for Services Leadership offers self-paced online courses in services leadership, developed by their academic faculty (http://www.webcitation.org/6ahAD1RMq).

Their courses are designed "for those interested in learning how to compete and grow through the use of service and services." The courses run concurrently every 8 weeks, and deal with topics such as:

- How to blueprint excellent customer experiences
- How to find and fix service quality gaps
- How to deliver front line service quality
- How to profit from service recovery
- How to innovate using the voice of the customer

CSL offers a certificate program in customer experience as well as tailor-made online courses to suit companies' needs.

The W. P. Carey Business School and their Centre for Services Leadership have become world-renowned for their leadership in the sciences of service.

## WHAT ARE iSCHOOLS TEACHING?

I published an exploratory study of managerial competencies for information professionals as taught in schools of information internationally (de Grandbois, 2013). In reviewing the curricula for courses in management in this sample, we also searched for Service Science, and found no offerings of this subject in information schools except for the three iSchools mentioned earlier—the University of California Berkeley, the Singapore Management University, and the University of Toronto.

I asked Dr. Robert Glushko, professor at the iSchool at the University of California, Berkeley, if there had been a change since Kelly Lyons's study. Here is what he answered:

> The Berkeley iSchool has a philosophy of not putting students into course tracks or programs, so it might be hard to find something that says "here are the courses you take if you want to study services" but we have several courses that are relevant. I teach a course called "Information Systems and Service Design" that is the primary one—and I even wrote a paper about its evolution over a multi-year period. We also have courses in Web Architecture/Web Services that are heavily infused with service design thinking.

In his 2011 paper Dr. Glushko adds,

> ... the iSchool perspective on the design and operation of service systems differs substantially from that in business or management schools and is also quite distinct from the more practical and enterprise oriented perspective in MIS programs (Lyons, 2010). The primary difference is that iSchools mix students with business, social science, engineering, or computer science undergraduate degrees in the same multi disciplinary courses
>
> *Glushko (2011)*

Then I asked Dr. Steven Miller, Dean of the School of Information Systems at the Singapore Management University, what they were doing in Service Science. Here is what he said:

> In our undergraduate programme, we have a "service systems and solutions" track. Relatively few students take the track, but a healthy number of students take the various electives within the track. Meaning—they are doing our "Service Science" courses—even though they might choose not to do the full track. We think this is fine. It is less important that they do the full track than they do the courses.
>
> At our undergraduate level—the whole philosophy of our BSc (IS Management) programme is Service Science. So by doing our Bachelors, even without doing the specific courses that are part of our Service Systems and Solutions track, they are doing things which are fully aligned with the SSME philosophy and strategies articulated to Jim Spohrer and others over the prior years.

> Our Master of IT in Business has two tracks—MITB (Financial Services), focused on processes, technology, operations, transformation, and evaluation of trade-offs across these aspects—deeply embedded in the context of banking, and MITB (Service Sector Analytics), focused on service sector processes, and applications of increasingly real-time analytics within these processes, along with enabling technology.
>
> We do not use the term "Service Science" for our MITB master's programme. But if you read over what the SSME principles are, and look at what we are doing, we are essentially instantiating SSME in a particular way in the two tracks of this master's programme.
>
> Purposely, we do not heavily promote "SSME" by itself. We do not proclaim ourselves as a "Service Science" place. But we are. In other words, rather than fly the flag of "Service Science," we just "do it," or do a particular variant of it that seems appropriate for our setting.

The iSchool at the University of Toronto gives students the opportunity to specialize in services and architecture in the field of information systems, media, and design, which includes a course on Service Science. This introductory course is available to master's level students across the areas of specialty within the iSchool. Students test Service Science concepts on service systems such as cultural and public institutions, nonprofits, and information-focused entities. The course description, learning outcomes, reading lists, and general information on how this course is taught can be found at http://www.webcitation.org/6ahBX31BD.

Applying an information lens to Service Science concepts has led to new research topics and directions:

> Our experience provides an example of how iSchools can bring impact and important diverse perspectives to studies in Service Science.
> 
> **Lyons (2010)**

Lyons maintains that

> It is no longer sufficient for people to have expertise in one area without understanding the connections and contexts of that expertise in relationship to other disciplines. This is especially true in a multidisciplinary field such as Service Science and in iSchools where information, technology, and people are of roughly equally significance such that knowledge and understanding in one (no matter how deep that knowledge reaches) is not sufficient without connections to the others.
>
> **Lyons (2010)**

Her study presents convincing reasons for participating in a Service Science research and education program.

## AN OUTSIDE OPINION

Schools of Information can be teaching Service Science, doing research in Service Science, and conducting conferences on Service Science for all of these reasons. This is a natural evolution in the study of information. Students need to be equipped for the economy in which they will live and work the next few decades. Let's not have them go to other faculties to keep up with our times.

The following questions have already been asked early on:

*Are LIS programs already leaders in the "Service Sciences"? Or, if they are not, could they be? Wouldn't it be wonderful if libraries were leading in handling technology change? LIS programs just might be able to make that happen.*

*Holt (2006)*

Holt goes on to say that

*By their very nature, schools of library and information science offer fertile fields to introduce and develop the "services sciences". Customer service has long been a staple in LIS courses, and information technology now is a strong study line or the central focus of LIS curricula.*

*Holt (2006)*

This was 2006. Lyons' study and proposal was published in 2010. It is now five years later—do we dare ask how far we have come?

## A SERVICE SCIENCE LOOK AT LIBRARIES

There is a case of Service Science studying libraries dating back to 1968. Philip Morse won the Lanchester prize of the Operations Research Society of America for his book on libraries as a service system (Morse, 1968). He attempted to apply management concepts such as performance measurement, statistical modeling, and queueing theory to library management situations, and wrote the book for both librarians and systems analysts.

Morse looked at the pattern of book use and how it changed with time, and at the problem of estimating and evaluating the degree to which the library satisfies or fails to satisfy the seeker of information. He included chapters on library use, probability distributions, arrivals and the Poisson distribution, queues and book circulation interference, and book use and the Markov process. He used the Science Library at MIT as an example of how his theories could be applied to library management.

In 2011, in the editorial column of the online journal *Service Science*, Richard Larson, from MIT, picks up on Morse's study to make a proposal for shared library delivery services based on the question "***Isn't it time for universities to say that all the millions of square feet allocated to books in library stacks also represent a relic of history?***" The italics and bold are his.

In case you are still wondering why information scientists should be involved in Service Science, please read the final paragraph of this editorial, which begins with this:

> As service scientists and engineers, paying attention to and even inventing new organizational forms for traditional service providers—forms that involve collaboration, sharing and even out-sourcing—may yield huge benefits in years to come

Larson's proposal can be considered as a serious option. But information professionals should be part of the conversation! The irony of the situation is that his article in Service Science is only available online, and only for a fee—unless of course you are fortunate to be part of a university that has a library that has purchased license agreements for this journal for its staff. Yes, everything is available on the Internet these days!

## MOVING ON

We have looked at the many synergies that exist between Service Science and the study of information. We have discussed the benefits of Service Science for the information professional and the schools that produce information professionals, including the benefits of partnerships, research, and redefining knowledge workers. We have examined the iSchool movement, enjoying its enthusiasm and its multidisciplinary focus, and have studied the reasons for its offering a home for Service Science. We looked briefly at what is being taught in Service Science, including in iSchools.

Next we'll look at the bigger picture of where Service Science is headed.

## REFERENCES

Apte, U., & Mason, R. (1995). Global Disaggregation of Information-Intensive Services. *Management Science, 41*(7), 1250–1262.
Bell, S. J., & Shank, J. (2007). *Academic librarianship by design: A blended librarian's guide to the tools and techniques* Chicago, IL: ALA.

Birchall, A. (2012). T-shaped people: the new employees of the digital age. *Management Today.* <http://www.webcitation.org/6ahByApSq> Accessed 21.01.15.

Brooks, K. (2012). <http://www.webcitation.org/6ahCT4P3m> Accessed 21.01.15.

Davenport, T. H., & Prusak, L. (1998). *Working Knowledge* Harvard Business School Press.

de Grandbois, Y. (2013). Managerial competencies for information professionals: an international perspective. *Library Review*, 62(4/5).

Fragnière, E., Nanchen, B., & Sitten, M. (2012). Ethnomethodology and theatre-based re-enactment in service design experiments. *Service Science*, 4(2).

Glushko, R. J. (2008). Designing a service science discipline with discipline. *IBM Systems Journal*, 47(1).

Glushko, R.J. (2011). The long and winding road to a course on service system design. *Art & science of service conference*. Berkeley: University of California.

Hansen, M.T. (2010). *An interview with IDEO CEO Tim Brown.* <http://www.webcitation.org/6ahDO1mXM> Accessed April 2015. Reprinted with permission, Chief Executive magazine/Chief Executive Group, (c) 2010.

He, S., & Wang, P. (2008). Applying service science to service innovation in library and information institutions. *Journal of Educational Media and Library Sciences*, 45(3), 367–370.

Holmberg, K., Tsou, A., & Sugimoto, C. R. (2013). The conceptual landscape of iSchools: examining current research interests of faculty members. *Information Research*, 18(3). paper C32. <http://www.webcitation.org/6ahDTYzgt> Accessed April 2015.

Holt, G. (2006). Holt's perspectives: publishing, libraries and "Service Sciences". *PLN*, December 5 (pp. 1–5).

Institute for the Future. (2011). *Future Work Skills* 2020. Palo Alto, CA.

Lusch, R. F., & Vargo, S. L. (2014). *Service-dominant logic: Premises, perspectives, possibilities* Cambridge, UK: Cambridge University Press.

Lyons, K. (2010). Service science in ischools. *iConference*, 2010, February 3–6, 2010. Urbana-Champaign, IL.

Maglio, P.. (2014). <http://cogsci.ucmerced.edu/sites/pmaglio/wp-content/uploads/sites/2/2014/11/mgmt150-syllabus.2014-DRAFT-6.pdf>.

Morse, P. (1968). *Library Effectiveness: A Systems Approach* Cambridge, MA: The MIT, Press.

Olson, G.M., & Grudin, J. (2009). The information school phenomenon. *ACM Interactions*, March and April.

Ostrom, A. L., Bitner, M. J., Brown, S. W., Burkhard, K. A., Goul, M., Smith-Daniels, V., et al. (2010). Moving forward and making a difference: research priorities for the science of service. *Journal of Service Research*, 13, 4. Originally published online 18 January 2010. <http://www.webcitation.org/6ahDrPpkf> Accessed April 2015.

Ostrom, A. L., Parasuraman, A., Bowen, DE., Patricio, L., & Voss, C. A. (2015). Service research priorities in a rapidly changing context. *Journal of Service Research*, 18(2), 127–159.

Swan, M. (2014). *iSchools: contemporary information technology theory studies.* <http://www.webcitation.org/6ahDzhVkE> Accessed April 2015.

Wu, D., He, D., Jiang, J., Dong, W., & Vo, K. T. (2012). The state of iSchools: an analysis of academic research and graduate education. *Journal of Information Science*, 38(1), 15–36.

# CHAPTER 4

# Service Science for a Smarter Planet

*There are no passengers on spaceship earth. We are all crew.*
*Marshall McLuhan*

## A SMARTER PLANET

Investigating a transdisciplinary field is an adventure because we are constantly learning about the connecting points between subjects. An engineer writing about Service Science would approach the topic from an engineering point of view, a business person from a management or financial point of view, a computer scientist from a technology point of view, social scientists from their points of view, and so on. It is inevitable that we learn about the other disciplines no matter which path we follow. Expanding our outlook in this way is an energizing and stimulating experience.

What I did not expect was the fact that this body of knowledge has a tremendous impact on making the world a better place. And this makes all the difference.

So how can Service Science have anything to do with the global financial crisis, climate change, crowded cities, pandemic threats, and health care? Is there a global model for the world's interdependent service systems? Can we create a next generation of citizens around the world who understand service systems? In other words, can there be a system of systems?

There is a beautiful video on YouTube (*System of Systems*, IBM Social Media) that describes the planet, when seen from space, as a neural network with its cities as its nodes. We can see the emergence of an electrical central nervous system. Natural systems, human systems, and physical objects have always emanated data, but we could not hear, see, or capture it. Because these entities are instrumented and interconnected, with technology, we now have access to this data. Devices such as sensors that measure temperature or traffic, the flow rates of water, or how much electricity is being used are all transmitting data. In fact, it is estimated that there are more *things* on the Internet than people. This phenomenon is called the Internet of Things (IoT).

With the emergence of a global data field we can now capture the data being emanated by human, natural, and physical objects. The analytics are derived from the data/information/knowledge/wisdom (DIKW) triangle, which has been written about extensively and is a familiar concept to the information professional.

> Data just is, it exists, it is factual and quantitative. By itself it has no meaning. It gains context to become Information by human interaction, thus putting it in a framework that allows understanding as to what the data represents. Information is qualitative. Information can be tacit, that which stays in our heads, or explicit, that which is expressed in different forms so that others can interact with it. When information is combined with experience, context, interpretation, reflection, ideas, and insights, it becomes knowledge. Knowledge, the ability to take an action, is created when information is transformed through human social interactions. Wisdom requires synthesis, often bringing together a wide range of knowledge created from information coming from a focused set of data. It is the ultimate understanding of the material and is the application that provides a strong common sense decision. It provides an organization with its strategy, correct judgments, and decisions. It cannot be captured like data, information, and knowledge can.

Ackoff, Russell L.(1989). From Data to Wisdom. *Journal of Applied Systems Analysis*, 3-9.

In the DIKW triangle, the bottom, largest part of the triangle is the data; going up one step is the information, then knowledge, then wisdom at the peak of the triangle. The analytics come about by applying intelligence to this data, transforming the data into information, then to knowledge and its application. A system of systems starts to emerge when all these elements are linked up, whether they are neurons, people, or cities.

We are finding more and more patterns in the data and more applications for the knowledge that is gleaned, both on an efficiency level and on a social, human network level.

We will now look briefly at the IoT, big data, analytics, cloud and cognitive computing as being the basis and the enablers of a smarter planet and smart cities.

## THE INTERNET OF THINGS

A decade ago, in their Internet Report 2005, the International Telecommunications Union first included the IoT (ITU, 2005), which spoke about the data field being emanated by physical objects. When short-range mobile transceivers were embedded into everyday items and gadgets, new ways of communication between people and things and between things themselves took place.

> *A new dimension has been added to the world of information and communication technologies (ICTs): from anytime, anyplace connectivity for anyone, we will now have connectivity for anything. Connections will multiply and create an entirely new dynamic network of networks—an Internet of Things. The Internet of Things is neither science fiction nor industry hype, but is based on solid technological advances and visions of network ubiquity that are zealously being realized.*
>
> *ITU (2005)*

The report predicted that because of integrated information processing, industrial products and everyday objects would take on smart characteristics and capabilities.

> *They may also take on electronic identities that can be queried remotely, or be equipped with sensors for detecting physical changes around them. Eventually, even particles as small as dust might be tagged and networked. Such developments will turn the merely static objects of today into newly dynamic things, embedding intelligence in our environment, and stimulating the creation of innovative products and entirely new services.*
>
> *ITU (2005)*

A few years later, at the European Commission Internet of Things Conference in Budapest, in May 2011, Dr. Lara Srivastava, who had edited the ITU report, gave a presentation on the IoT entitled "Back to the Future" (Srivastava, 2011). She explains the IoT in a highly entertaining, informative way. The predictions of 2005 were now a reality. She gives four key technology enablers underlying the IoT vision: the ability of tagging things through technologies like, for example, RFID, sensing things through sensors and actuators, shrinking things through advances in miniaturization and nanotechnology, and things that think through increasingly embedded processing power.

Complementary developments such as embedded intelligence in smart cities and homes, real-time monitoring in medical and environmental contexts, augmented reality such as memory enhancements and the link between the semantic web or Web 3.0 and the IoT, pushed this idea forward. It was now possible to link systems, datasets, and objects that were not previously connected.

## IoT COMES ON STAGE

Ten years after the ITU report, the *Wall Street Journal* (March 2015) reported that the IoT took center stage at CeBIT, a major IT fair in Hanover, Germany. They described adding sensing, computing, and communications capability to all kinds of hardware. They gave five examples of the coming connected world.

1. Robochop is an assembly line of industrial robots that make sculptures from foam cubes according to designs submitted via a smartphone app.
2. Deutsche Telekom and Canyon Bicycles have partnered on a bike that calls an ambulance in case of an accident, and tells the owner its location if stolen.
3. The Claas tractor has sensors that measure nitrogen levels in plants, determining the exact amount of fertilizer required, and then dispenses that fertilizer from a device on the tractor's rear.
4. Dornbracht's digitally controlled bathroom lets the user choose bath water temperature with an app. The app also alerts the user when the tub is full.
5. A Durkopp Adler sewing machine for factory use is equipped with an Internet connection that allows operators to measure its effectiveness and make changes as necessary. The Internet connection also allows the transmission of embroidery patterns direct to the machine.

The IoT was everywhere. Soon the Council of the IoT was established. The purpose of Council is to follow and forecast what will happen when smart objects surround us in smart homes, offices, streets, and cities.

> IoT is a paradigm shift and an ontological change. Our very notions of what it means to be human and what it means to be in the world are based on subject—object dichotomies. IoT brings a third party into the equation, a database, algos and scenario reality that is always present in any interaction between object and subject. This is not an indifferent reality, however, but one of real stakeholders and investors.
>
> *http://www.webcitation.org/6ahLhYYc4*

The Council describes the IoT as the seamless flow between the:
- BAN *(body area network)*: the ambient hearing aide, the smart t-shirts...
- LAN *(local area network)*: the smart meter as a home interface...
- WAN *(wide area network)*: the bike, car, train, bus, drone...
- VWAN *(very wide area network)*: the "wise" city as e-gov services everywhere no longer tied to physical locations.

## OTHER PRACTICAL APPLICATIONS

Daniel Burrus, considered one of the world's leading technology forecasters and innovation experts and the founder and CEO of Burrus Research, gives this example of a practical application of the IoT.

He recounts how a bridge collapsed in Minnesota in 2007, killing many people. The steel girders were no longer able to sustain the load on the bridge. If we use smart cement when building or repairing bridges (i.e., cement with sensors built in), the cement can warn us of coming danger zones like stresses, cracks, and warps. These can be repaired before a catastrophe happens. In addition, these sensors can detect ice on the bridge and communicate this information to your car, which will tell you to slow down. If you don't, the car will slow down by itself.

> *This isn't just about money savings. It's not about bridges, and it's not about cities. This is a huge and fundamental shift. When we start making things intelligent, it's going to be a major engine for creating new products and new services.*
>
> *Burrus (2014)*

A myriad of applications of how the IoT can be applied in homes, cities, industries, and bodies can be found in many sites on the Web—for example, the connected home, the connected industry, the connected company, and so on.

If you are interested in seeing how the IoT came to be, Postscapes.com (http://postscapes.com/internet-of-things-history. Accessed March 2015) gives a wonderful history of the IoT, starting with the electromagnetic telegraph in 1832 and going right to today where new projects, Twitter posts, interviews, events, presentations, videos, and IoT news are added daily.

## EARLY THOUGHT LEADERS

I would like to acknowledge three great visionaries that had ideas that were precursors to the IoT, from the Postscapes website, with permission.

> *1926*: Nikola Tesla in an interview with Colliers magazine said:
>
> *When wireless is perfectly applied the whole earth will be converted into a huge brain, which in fact it is, all things being particles of a real and rhythmic whole…and the instruments through which we shall be able to do this will be amazingly simple compared with our present telephone. A man will be able to carry one in his vest pocket.*

> *1950*: Alan Turing in his article *Computing Machinery and Intelligence* in the *Oxford Mind Journal* (Via @Kevin Ashton) said:
>
> *…It can also be maintained that it is best to provide the machine with the best sense organs that money can buy, and then teach it to understand and speak English. This process could follow the normal teaching of a child.*

> *1964*: In *Understanding Media* Marshall McLuhan stated:
>
> *…by means of electric media, we set up a dynamic by which all previous technologies—including cities—will be translated into information systems.*

Even the journal *Foreign Affairs* (2014) ran an article on the IoT stating that linking the digital and physical worlds will have profound implications for both. In the section on The Connected Life, the IoT is described from the point of view of energy efficiency, health care, smart houses, smart cities, weather, agricultural inputs, and pollution levels.

> The ultimate realization of the Internet of Things will be to transmit actual things through the Internet. Users can already send descriptions of objects that can be made with personal digital fabrication tools, such as 3-D printers and laser cutters. As data turn into things and things into data, long manufacturing supply chains can be replaced by a process of shipping data over the Internet to local production facilities that would make objects on demand, where and when they were needed.
>
> *Gershenfeld & Vasseur (2014)*

A recent *Business Insider* article claims that the IoT market will soon be bigger than the PC, smartphone, and tablet markets combined (Greenough, 2015).

This information is in the form of a slideshow highlighting the most important ways the Internet of Everything market will develop and the benefits newly connected devices will offer consumers and businesses.

The 2015 *Horizon Report*, produced by the Educause Learning Initiative, annually describes six areas of emerging technology that will have significant impact on higher education and creative expression over the next 1–5 years. The IoT has been cited as an area of important development in both 2012 and 2015. Examples of applications of the IoT are given across several disciplines, including using student cards embedded with RFID tags to track their class attendance.

We have seen that the IoT is here and that its applications are growing every day. The fact that everything will be on the Internet leads to the question, how will we deal with the data that is being generated by this unprecedented influx into the virtual arena? The answer lies within the realm of big data and analytics.

## BIG DATA

This capacity to connect and integrate isolated data leads to an even more gigantic amount of data in the world, growing at a compound annual rate of 60% and gaining speed all the time. In terms of quantifying data we have gone from bits to bytes to yottabytes in a few decades. In the hierarchy of big data, there are petabytes, exabytes, zettabytes, and yottabytes. The challenge is one of coming to agreement on the right words to describe what lies beyond a yottabyte, which is septillion bytes.

Analyzing large data sets—named big data—is becoming a basis of competition, underpinning new waves of productivity growth, services innovation, and consumer surplus, according to research done by the McKinsey Global Institute and McKinsey's Business Technology Office (McKinsey Global Institute, 2011). They report that leaders in every sector will have to grapple with the implications of big data. The increasing volume and detail of information captured by enterprises, the rise of multimedia, social media, and the IoT will fuel exponential growth in data for the foreseeable future.

For example, Wal-Mart, a retail giant, handles more than 1 million customer transactions every hour, feeding databases estimated at more than 2.5 petabytes—the equivalent of 167 times the books in America's Library of Congress. Facebook, a social-networking website, is home to 40 billion photos. These transactions are simply data, however when analytics are applied, patterns emerge that contain practical and predictive information about the customer. Another example is the decoding of the human genome, involving analyzing 3 billion base pairs. This took 10 years the first time it was done in 2003, but can now be achieved in 1 week (Cukier, 2010).

McKinsey's 2011 report, *Big data: the next frontier for innovation*, is a good introduction to this development. By 2014 and 2015 McKinsey was reporting a "fait accompli" with articles such as:

"How to get the most from big data" http://www.webcitation.org/6ahOdy8r2.

"Getting big impact from big data" http://www.webcitation.org/6ahOjxdJx.

"Power to the new people analytics" http://www.webcitation.org/6ahOpmUnW. Accessed April 2015.

An excellent primer on big data and analytics, short, easy to read, and full of interesting, accurate information is Thomas Davenport's book, *Big Data at Work* (2014).

Big data is becoming a means to gain commercial advantage for companies on the leading edge of using it. However, there are other uses for it as well.

## NOT ONLY BIG BUSINESS

Digital pioneers, for example Sir Tim Berners-Lee, inventor of the World Wide Web, see the potential to turn this mass of data into a positive power for the consumer. Examples of this exist already, such as the United Kingdom's Opening Up government website (http://www.webcitation.org/6ahOy3S5Q), which provides consumers with a range of local information based on data sources that would once have been stored and unavailable.

Berners-Lee is not in favor of ownership of big data. In a 2014 interview with The Guardian he said, "The data we create about ourselves should be owned by each of us, not by the large companies that harvest it." Berners-Lee told the IPExpo Europe 2014 in London that the potential of big data will be wasted as its current owners use it to serve ever more "queasy" targeted advertising. By gaining access to their own data, people could use it with information about themselves from other sources in order to create "rich data"—a far more valuable commodity than mere "big data."

According to Tim Berners-Lee, "If a computer collated data from your doctor, your credit card company, your smart home, your social networks, and so on, it could get a real overview of your life." Berners-Lee was visibly enthusiastic about the potential applications of that knowledge, from living more healthily to picking better Christmas presents for his nephews and nieces. This, he said, would be "rich data" (Turk, 2014).

Berners-Lee is also an important participant in The MIT Computer Science and Artificial Intelligence Laboratory—known as CSAIL—the largest research laboratory at MIT and one of the world's most important centers of information technology research. See http://www.webcitation.org/6ahP6AD7f.

An example of big data being used for scientific purposes has been developed by the CERN, and is called the Worldwide LHC Computing Grid (WLCG). The Grid is a gigantic amount of computer power and data storage capacity, and it's based on the same idea as the Web—the ability to share information between computers in geographically different locations. The difference is whereas the Web shares the information that is on the computers, the Grid also shares computing power and storage capacity. Scientists log on to the Grid from their personal computers and are able to very quickly carry out complex calculations that are way beyond the capacity of their PCs.

The CERN had a need for the processing of extremely large and complex operations, and therefore invested in the development of the Grid. According to the CERN website (http://www.webcitation.org/6ahPReEvg), their new particle accelerator alone, the Large Hadron

Collider (LHC), purported to be the world's largest scientific instrument, produces nearly 1% of all the digital information produced annually on the planet, equivalent to 15 million gigabytes. Hundreds of partners around the world are able to process huge quantities of experimental data, as the Grid connects the power of thousands of computer centers into a seamless whole. This technology relies on a multilayered software structure that feeds data toward thousands of computers dispersed around the world and collects the results. WLCG serves a community of more than 8,000 physicists around the world with near real-time access to LHC data, and the power to process it. On July 4, 2012 Grid results allowed the CERN to announce the discovery of a new boson, the Higgs boson, also known as the God particle.

## ANALYTICS

In simple terms analytics means using quantitative methods to derive insights from data, and then drawing on those insights to shape business decisions and, ultimately, to improve business performance (Rich & Harris, 2010).

In the same way that your online presence attracts all kinds of businesses to your in-box, retailers and industries are going for the same type of marketing and sales opportunities in their actual, not virtual stores in a tactile manner. Big data supplies data that can be analyzed to find what you buy, when, how often, which brands, before, after, or during browsing in the store, and so on. Businesses are scrambling to be early adopters of the application of analytics to their customers' habits and needs. To illustrate, the following ad is seen on the Google Analytics page (http://www.webcitation.org/6ahPY6ObE):

> Your customers go everywhere; shouldn't your analytics? Google Analytics shows you the full customer picture across ads and videos, websites and social tools, tablets and smartphones. That makes it easier to serve your current customers and win new ones.

Analytics can be descriptive—for example, demographic information such as where the customer lives, how many family members he has, what the value of his home is, what his monthly salary is, etc. Then, what products did the customer buy last week, how much did he spend, what sales promotions did he respond to, how much has he spent over the last month, year, 5 years?

Analytics can also be predictive—based on the descriptive data, predictions can be made on the likelihood of that customer responding to different promotions, buying a product, buying another product in conjunction with the first one, how much the customer is likely to spend over the next quarter.

*Thus predictive analytics is emerging as a game-changer. Instead of looking backward to analyze "what happened?" predictive analytics help executives answer "What"s next?' and "What should we do about it?".*

**Rich and Harris (2010)**

Analytics are also prescriptive—making specific, actionable recommendations based on the descriptive data and the predictive calculations or suppositions.

An interesting example of the use of analytics was provided by the United Kingdom's Royal Shakespeare Co., who used analytics to look at its audience members' names, addresses, performances attended, and prices paid for tickets over a period of 7 years. The theater company then developed a marketing program that increased regular attendees by more than 70% and its membership by 40% (Rich & Harris, 2010).

## CLOUD COMPUTING

Cloud computing is a way to deliver any technology or business process as a digital service. Cloud computing uses the Internet as a platform to collect, store, and process data. Amazon, Google, Microsoft, and others lease computer power to clients who have on-demand IT resources and services via the Internet, with pay-as-you-go pricing. This is much easier and cheaper than buying expensive equipment. You can access as many resources as you need, instantly, and only pay for what you use. Cloud computing services can be private, public, or hybrid. Private cloud (also called internal cloud, or corporate cloud) services can deliver information from a company's data center to internal users, ensuring control by the company as well as security trust. In the public cloud, a third party delivers the services over the Internet. Major public cloud providers include Amazon Web Services, Microsoft Azure, IBM/SoftLayer, and Google Compute Engine.

Hybrid cloud is a combination of public and private cloud services, with operability between the two if necessary. Companies can run secure confidential applications on the private cloud while using the public cloud for other work that is not sensitive. The hybrid cloud takes advantage of all that a public cloud infrastructure can provide, while maintaining control over critical data that is available only to those involved.

Cloud computing is divided into three broad service categories: infrastructure as a service, platform as a service, and software as service. Further reliable information on cloud computing and other technology topics can be found at Tech target, which is a network of technology-specific websites with independent content and analysis: http://www.webcitation.org/6ahPfccj7.

## COGNITIVE COMPUTING

Of all the trends that are happening, the era of cognitive computing is the one I find the most exciting and significant, that will usher in the next leap of innovation.

Cognitive computing is a major technology trend that has important implications for service system improvement. We are now teaching computers how to think, and the result of this engagement is the bettering of results that we get from only humans, or only computers.

A computer named Watson has captured the public's imagination and has introduced us to the cognitive era. If you have not heard of Watson, please see the following: http://www.webcitation.org/6ahR3cvX2.

Watson is a computer that became famous because he won over the top human candidate of an American quiz show called Jeopardy. He is the friend of the information specialist. Imagine finding a TED talk that was related to 10 other TED talks by the concepts and ideas in the talk. Watson has succeeded in indexing all the TED talks. You can check it out on http://www.webcitation.org/6aqXiepX5.

There is of course much more to Watson than this. IBM has identified three types of capabilities for cognitive systems: engagement, decision, and discovery.

Engagement is the manner in which humans and computer systems interact and how this significantly augments the capacity to achieve results neither could achieve alone. These systems have decision-making abilities that constantly change when new information is added and are based on evidence. These systems can also discover new ideas, new insights that have not been thought of before. There are solutions to problems in papers and research that were never published. Watson has the capacity to take it all in and find the hidden jewel. The implications for medicine, the environment, and health are enormous. In fact, every field of endeavor will be enhanced by the new permutations and combinations that could not be seen before. New services, new solutions, new ways of doing things. This is an area that we can participate in with ease.

## THE CIRCULAR ECONOMY

This is also prerequisite to appreciating the arrival of a smarter planet, and merits a place here, however brief. A circular economy would mean the end of planned obsolescence. This means re-using, repairing, refurbishing, and recycling existing materials and products. What used to be regarded as "waste" can be turned into a resource.

Sources of future economic growth would be more products made out of secondary raw materials, and waste would be considered a valuable resource. New business models would retain physical goods longer and more efficiently in productive use. We would rent appliances rather than buy them, and the manufacturers would take back our old machines to recycle parts into new ones. Even manufacturing would become an information service in the circular economy of the future.

The Ellen MacArthur Foundation has put the following beautiful explanations of the circular economy on YouTube:

http://www.webcitation.org/6aqXudebF
http://www.webcitation.org/6aqYDXqnQ

And the European Commission has begun an ambitious strategy for the circular economy for late 2015:

http://www.webcitation.org/6aqYPmopl

## SMARTER PLANET INITIATIVE

The coming of the IoT, big data, analytics, cloud and cognitive computing, as well as the circular economy, has many applications and repercussions. Things have become smart, and analytics have made data intelligible and applicable in a multitude of contexts that are growing exponentially.

This capacity has enabled us to apply service systems thinking to actual world problems. The Smarter Planet Initiative is one such avenue. Again, this is IBM. The importance and scale of this type of initiative is so far-reaching that it has its place in this discussion.

We have seen that real life service systems such as cities, health care institutions, transportation, and food and energy networks are combinations of people, organizations, and information and technologies performing services that produce a particular result. We need more livable cities, better health care systems, more sustainable food and water supplies, and greener energy systems. The Smarter Planet Initiative posits that this can be done with the technology and the information that we have available today. The Smarter Planet Initiative actually *demands* a multidisciplinary perspective.

The Smarter Planet Initiative is based on the fact that, as we have seen, digital intelligence is being infused into the service systems and processes that make the world work—cars, appliances, roads, power grids, even clothing and water. Trillions of digital devices connected through the Internet are producing an ocean of data. All of this information, from the flow of markets to the pulse of societies, can be turned into knowledge because we now have the computational power and advanced analytics to make sense of it. With this knowledge we can reduce costs, cut waste, and improve the efficiency, productivity, and quality of everything from companies to cities.

IBM launched the Smarter Planet Initiative in 2009. The Smarter Planet umbrella includes Smarter Planet Initiatives such as Smarter Buildings, Smarter Government, Smarter Cities, Smarter Commerce, and Smarter Health Care. There are more than 21 Smarter Planet themes. For example, the Smarter Food program includes projects that seek to improve agricultural yields, reduce waste, and improve sustainability. Other themes include smarter buildings, commerce, communications, education, energy, government, health care, public safety, retail, security, traffic, and transportation systems. Ann Rubin, IBM's VP Branded Content and Global Creative reported that:

> Smarter Planet is still our point of view on the world, but now it's about the "how", showing people are literally making value in new ways with IBM technology.... It's about taking Smarter Planet to the next level.
> 
> *Rubin (2014)*[1]

A quick and fun way to learn about the Smarter Planet Initiative is to go to YouTube and begin with a few introductory videos. You may want to begin by viewing *System of Systems* http://www.webcitation.org/6ahRV8xE1 and *The Internet of Things*, http://www.webcitation.org/6ahRl0cpZ and going from there to a good general introduction to Smarter Planet such as http://www.webcitation.org/6ahRqKmJb.

And a good way to keep up with the Smarter Planet Initiative's new and exciting developments is the Smarter Planet Blog: Building a Smarter Planet, at http://www.webcitation.org/6ahRyEhAW.

---

[1] Reprint Courtesy of International Business Machines Corporation, © 2014 International Business Machines Corporation.

This blog:

> is a platform for the discussion of topics and points of view related to IBM's Smarter Planet Initiatives. Through the blog, we seek to engage a global audience in thoughtful dialogue around the idea of leveraging smarter technologies to improve the world in which we live.[2]

Posts on this blog are so interesting and wide-ranging it's a pleasure to see good news of good happenings in our smarter world.

## ANOTHER OPINION

Tom Kucharvy is founder of Beyond IT Inc, which describes itself as a market strategy and consulting firm that helps companies manage the transition to a global knowledge economy. Here is how he describes the Smarter Planet Initiative:

> IBM's huge, corporate-wide Smarter Planet Initiative is, in many ways, the application of SSME to critical, real-world problems. SSME, after all, is an effort to create a science around decomposing and recomposing service-based processes, optimizing service supply chains and value chains and creating interdisciplinary research centers to design and optimize complex "service systems"—combinations of people, organizational networks and technologies that are aligned around a specific objective, such as designing and managing more liveable cities, more effective healthcare systems and more efficient energy networks.
>
> This effectively transforms SSME from an academic discipline into an instrument for addressing societal needs. It provides universities with the tools required to create education tracks and, eventually, degree programs around social goals—thereby attracting and making it easier for students who want to "change the world."
>
> Kucharvy (2010)

## SMARTER CITIES

The United Nations Population Fund (UNFPA Website) reports that the world is undergoing the largest wave of urban growth in history. As long ago as 2008, more than half of the world's population were already living in towns and cities. By 2030 this number is expected to expand to almost 5 billion. While mega-cities have captured much public attention, most of the new growth will occur in smaller towns and cities, which have fewer resources to respond to the magnitude of the change.

---

[2] Reprint Courtesy of International Business Machines Corporation, © 2014 International Business Machines Corporation.

As millions move into cities, multiple systems and infrastructures need to become more intelligent. There will be a greater demand for vital services such as health care, safety, better education, accessible governments, clean water, and energy from renewable sources.

Smarter Cities, obviously, are part of the Smarter Planet Initiative. A city is a living environment of different cultures, ideas, and systems that are interdependent.

> Smarter Cities mean safe neighbourhoods, quality schooling, affordable housing, traffic that flows. This initiative looks at how the systems in a city can interact to make a city a better, healthier place for people to live, a place where businesses thrive and prosper, the economy is sustainable and the population happy and healthy.
> 
> **IBM Social Media**[3]

We have the technologies to enable us to live much better, to change the way in which businesses and people operate. Eco-system services, collaboration tools, and information let people work together in new and effective ways. We have social needs, and we need to be in a community with a low carbon footprint and a high quality of life. A smarter city can do this. Smarter cities of all sizes are capitalizing on new technologies and insights to transform their systems, operations, and service delivery.

See the following examples:

> For this we must look to the city within the city, interconnected systems that undergird a city—stretching into roads, utilities, and water supplies. These systems are intelligent in that they have software and sensors embedded everywhere. Taking the example of improving traffic flows, Singapore, Stockholm and Brisbane have gone ahead with Smarter Traffic, where all the information concerning traffic flows have been fed into computers and analyzed in order to ascertain the best time and location movement of their traffic. They have seen significant drops in congestion and pollution. Italy, Malta, Texas and Australia have begun using smart meters for their power grids, saving their citizens a hefty percentage of their utility bills. There is also the well known example of the New York Police Department using a real time crime centre to apprehend criminals, resulting in a 30% reduction in their crime rates. Other examples are hospitals ensuring that the same information follows the patient through all the different departments, city governments streamlining information or schools ensuring all areas get the same quality of education.
> 
> **IBM Social Media**

These solutions implement existing IBM technology such as IBM cloud computing, analytics, mobility, and social business.

---

[3] Reprint Courtesy of International Business Machines Corporation, © 2014 International Business Machines Corporation.

Videos such as Introducing the Smarter City series, which includes Tale of a Smarter City, and City of Dreams, uploaded by IBM Social Media, explain smarter cities very well. There is so much that can be followed up by related videos that you will need discipline to pull yourself away!

To see the best on how to build a smarter city, see Ginni Rommety, IBM: http://www.webcitation.org/6ahS92ByP.

To see a playlist on smarter cities videos, see: http://www.webcitation.org/6ahSDvsxf.

Go here: http://www.webcitation.org/6ahSL6vJp to get the idea of smarter cities from real people in real cities. On May 15, 2015, for example, I could see short videos from the Smart City Library on Miami-Dade County, Sheltering a City with data: the Rio de Janiero Story, Honolulu Citizens Building a Smarter City. This access point is updated very often, so you always have new material.

A 2015 report, *Using Innovation and Technology to Improve City Services* by Sherri Greenberg, identifies key trends that are driving cities to break out of the old business-as-usual models. Sherri Greenberg is a public policy professor at the University of Texas at Austin. Increasingly, cities are the public sector service delivery engines in the United States. They have heard a call to action: residents expect cities to find ways to improve services and cities are gearing up to do so. City governments, residents, and interest groups are actively seeking methods for better service delivery. This report examines how cities are using innovative policies, governance structures, and technologies to improve city services.

We collect and analyze information. Analytics and new reporting tools can now sift through mountains of data to find the gem of intelligence and knowledge. It is this gem that provides the key to the solution to problems faced in cities all over the world.

A few examples around the world of using Smarter Cities technology are Rio de Janeiro; New Taipei; Tucson, Arizona; and Digital Delta in Holland.

Frost & Sullivan is an independent global research organization of 1,800 analysts and consultants who monitor more than 300 industries and 250,000 companies. In 2014 their independent analysis confirmed that IBM is the leading Smart City integrator. They awarded IBM their Visionary Innovation Leadership Award as the Best-in-Class Smart City Integrator Global 2014. This was based on projects with city governments to provide the technologies that can monitor traffic congestion, save energy in buildings and to show what the impact of smart cities can accomplish.

IBM focuses on collecting data and leveraging its own technologies, such as cloud services, Big Data analytics, mobile and social, and its Intelligent Operations Center to integrate city systems and allow for the efficient management of city resources.

## OTHER CONCEPTS OF WHOLE SERVICE CITIES

Smart cities deal with improving existing systems, or putting in new ones to cities that need them. There are other concepts coming out that deal with building cities from scratch.

Whole service refers to three categories of service capabilities necessary for quality of life for people inside service systems: *flows* (transportation, water/air, food/products, energy, information/communications), *development* (buildings/shelter, retail/hospitality/entertainment/culture, finance, health, education), and *governance* (rules that make competing for collaborators co-elevating) (Spohrer, 2010).

An example of whole service is the notion of the start-up city. The principle lies in the fact that it might be faster and more efficient to build a city with all its infrastructure and governance than to fix an existing one. According to Paul Romer (2015), an American economist, entrepreneur, and activist, this is a feasible solution described in the concept of his Charter Cities Initiative. This idea addresses poverty by asking for an unoccupied piece of land and a charter, which will delineate governance, rules for security, and economic opportunities for a better quality of life.

The discussion on creating whole cities from scratch may seem to be way out there, and the charter cities idea has certainly engendered a lot of controversy. This idea is one to be cognizant of in the next few years.

However, for the record, this is not a new concept—consider Hong Kong. The land was given by China, and the rules, basic infrastructure, and market economy were put in place by Britain. Singapore has already created two new cities in China, and nations like Singapore and South Korea want to export their city-building expertise to other countries.

Building floating cities on the ocean is another whole service idea that is being proposed by Patri Friedman, grandson of the economist Milton Friedman. He has co-founded the Seasteading Institute, and is promoting the testing of new ideas for governing society.

*The world needs a place where those who wish to experiment with building new societies can go to test out their ideas. All land is already claimed—which makes the oceans humanity's next frontier.*

*(http://www.webcitation.org/6ahSQMBI5)*

## MAKING A DIFFERENCE

*Slowly, but surely the world view that businesses, cities, nations are all service systems is taking hold. And what is exciting to service scientists, those who study service systems, is that like agriculture "getting good at" growing crops and like manufacturing "getting good at" producing products, finally in human-history we are "getting good at" designing service systems.*

*Spohrer (2010)*

We mentioned earlier the study done at the W. P. Carey School of Business at Arizona State University that established 10 priorities for research in Service Science. One of the priorities is transformative service research (TSR), which targets the improvement of consumer and societal welfare through service. This research centers on creating uplifting changes and improvements in the well-being of both individuals and communities:

*TSR seeks to better the quality of life of present and future generations of consumers and citizens through services. As such, it examines aspects such as the social and ecological consequences and benefits of services offerings, increased access to valued services, the disparity in the quality of service offerings to different groups, the design and cocreation of services with consumers that honours both the agency and the cultural values of individuals and communities, the identification of and planning for the impact of services on well-being and sustainability, and the impact of consumers' service experiences on well-being.*

*Ostrom et al. (2010)*

This exciting new wave of knowledge keeps coming in. This chapter has shown its stream flowing into a larger base, one that incorporates urban planning, engineering, and architecture, as well as governance of cities, regions, and nations.

## SERVICE SCIENCE AND SOCIAL VALUE

Social value has become a popular buzzword, though the concept has been around for some time in terms of sustainability and corporate social responsibility. It asks the question, what contribution to society do community projects and businesses make?

The appeal of measuring this social value (or impact) is that economic valuation techniques can be used and therefore hard answers can be given (Henriques, 2014).

What is the Service Science perspective of social value? An exciting take on this topic is the first chapter of a recently published book, *Service Systems Science* (Kijima, ed. 2015), which is Part Two of the Translational Systems Sciences series published by Springer Japan.

Authors of this first chapter, Spohrer, Demirkan, and Lyons begin with a comprehensive overview of social value based on Mulgan (2010). Service entities such as nonprofits, governments, and funding agencies need to be able to measure the social value of their contribution and many competing methods for doing so have appeared in the last 40 years.

Mulgan summarizes the main methods of measuring social value, including cost/benefits, stated/revealed preferences, social return on investment, value-added assessments, quality of life/satisfaction, government accounting measures, and field-specific measures. However, he also maintains that it is a misconception to measure social value as being only objective, fixed, and stable. It is when social value is seen as subjective, changeable, and dynamic that appropriate metrics can be defined. Social, psychological, and environmental factors are needed in addition to the traditional economic principles.

Information professionals: here is a way to measure the incredibly rich social value we harbor as knowledge workers! This Service Science perspective article came in as we were going to press, but I want you to be aware of this even though it cannot be thoroughly discussed here.

## INSTRUMENTED, INTERCONNECTED, INTELLIGENT

A good way to end this chapter on the smarter planet is to show you this wonderful blog post written by Bill Chamberlin, Emerging Tech Trends Analyst, IBM Market Research (2014).[4] He is describing how the world's systems are becoming more instrumented, interconnected, and intelligent. Instrumented in that information is captured wherever it exists, such as through the use of remote sensors. Interconnected as information is moved from where it is collected to wherever it can be usefully

---

[4] Reprint Courtesy of International Business Machines Corporation, © 2014 International Business Machines Corporation.

consumed. And intelligent in that information is processed, analyzed, and acted upon to derive greater knowledge and value.

He goes on to say: ...

> Our planet Earth could be covered in an Internet of Things, but without the ability to create intelligence, it will never become a Smarter Planet.
> Intelligence does not happen just by embedding sensors and computers in objects and then connecting those objects to the Internet. Making the world smarter requires gathering all of the data that is observed and collected by the 'things', analyzing that data (either at the device level or via analytics capability in the cloud), and then making decisions that improve businesses, industries and society.
> To make sense of all the data that will be captured, we need sophisticated big data, analytics and cognitive computing systems that turn all the data into intelligence. This intelligence will allow us to become smarter....to help us reduce cost and waste, improve efficiency and productivity, and raise the quality of everything from our products, to our companies, to our cities.
> When instrumentation and interconnectedness is combined with intelligence, it can lead to unprecedented real-time visibility into our business processes, systems, infrastructures, and entire supply chains. So, while the emerging concept of an Internet of Things is a critical foundation for a Smarter Planet, we need to make sure that we don't forget the third "I". An intelligent Internet of Things will enable us to create a Smarter Planet that is much greener, more efficient, more comfortable and safer.[5]

In this chapter we have looked at the connections between Service Science and the latest technology trends—all of which converge on the smarter planet and quality of life initiatives. There are so many new developments, and they keep coming. It is marvelous to be in the information sector where we have the pleasure as well as the duty to keep up with all of this.

We have the systems, the science, and the will to make this good and loving world a better place. I think we could have reached this conclusion from any topic we would have wanted to cover. We came to it from the study of Service Science.

In the next chapter, let us give a little credit where credit is due in the story of this rapid and never-ending stream of knowledge called Service Science. We will also look at the community of professional and academic associations that have sprung up, and that communicate with their members and with others in a very transdisciplinary and T-shaped way. We will end the chapter with interview questions that ask about smart universities, jobs of the future, and where Service Science is headed.

---

[5] Reprint Courtesy of International Business Machines Corporation, © 2014 International Business Machines Corporation.

# REFERENCES

Berners-Lee, S.T. (2014). <http://www.webcitation.org/6ahSXQ8zZ>. Accessed 20.03.15.
Burrus, D. (2014). *The internet of things is far bigger than anyone realizes.* <http://www.webcitation.org/6ahSftXOE>. Accessed April 2015.
Centre for Services Leadership. (2010). WP Carey School of Business, Arizona State University. *Business report.* <http://www.webcitation.org/6ahSoge3P>. Accessed April 2015.
Chamberlin, B. (2014). Blog post: <http://www.webcitation.org/6ahT2mu1o> Accessed April 2015.[6]
Council of the Internet of Things. <http://www.theinternetofthings.eu/>. Accessed July 2015.
Cukier, K. (2010). Data, data everywhere. *The Economist.* <http://www.webcitation.org/6ahT9OIbM>.
Davenport, T. (2014). *Big data at work: Dispelling the myths, uncovering the opportunities.* Boston, MA: Harvard Business Review Press.
Frost & Sullivan. (2014). <http://www.webcitation.org/6ahTKz6hf>. Accessed April 2015.
Gershenfeld, N., & Vasseur, J.P. (2014). As objects go online; the promise (and pitfalls) of the internet of things. *Foreign Affairs*, March–April. <http://www.webcitation.org/6ahTQVbSL>. Accessed April 2015.
Greenberg, S. (2015). *Using innovation and technology to improve city services.* <http://www.webcitation.org/6ahTdR2Vh>. Accessed April 2015.
Greenough, J. (2015). <http://www.webcitation.org/6ahTkL3hD>. Accessed May 2015.
Henriques, A. (2014). Social value: a sustainability buzzword without a meaning? The Guardian. <http://www.webcitation.org/6ahTsxcx0>. Accessed 26 March 2015.
Horizon Report. (2015). <http://www.webcitation.org/6ahTy5pIm>. Accessed March 2015.
IBMSmarterPlanetUK. *Introducing the smarter city, no. 1 in a series.* <http://www.webcitation.org/6ahU3uMSP>.[7]
IBM Social Media. *Smarter planet.* <http://www.webcitation.org/6ahU9zDx2>.[7]
IBM Social Media. *System of systems.* <http://www.webcitation.org/6aldaonQ3>.[7]
IBM Social Media. *The internet of things.* <http://www.webcitation.org/6ale2TNsC>.[7]
IBM Social Media. *Tale of a smarter city.* <http://www.webcitation.org/6aleM6WVz>.[7]
IBM Social Media. *Smarter cities playlist.* <http://www.webcitation.org/6aleWXV6d>.[7]
International Telecommunications Union (ITU). (2005). <http://www.webcitation.org/6aletRJOG>.
Kijima, K. (Ed.), (2015). Service systems science. Series: Translational systems sciences (Vol. 2). Japan: Springer.
Kucharvy, T. (2010). IBM's Plan to Transform University IT Education: And Spur Student Enthusiasm in the Process. <http://service-science.info/wp-content/uploads/2010/05/2010_02-IBM-SSME-final.pdf>. Accessed April 2015.
McKinsey Global Institute. (2011). <http://www.webcitation.org/6alhg5s1E>.
Mulgan, G. (2010). Measuring social value. *Stanford Social Innovation Review,* Summer Issue. (pp. 37–43). <http://www.webcitation.org/6alhsQKYQ>. Accessed March 2015.

---

[6] Reprint Courtesy of International Business Machines Corporation, © 2014 International Business Machines Corporation.

[7] Reprint Courtesy of International Business Machines Corporation, © 2014 International Business Machines Corporation.

Ostrom, A. L., Bitner, M. J., Brown, S. W., Burkhard, K. A., Goul, M., Smith-Daniels, V., et al. (2010). Moving forward and making a difference: research priorities for the science of service. *Journal of Service Research, 13*, 4 . 2010. Originally published online 18 January 2010. <http://www.webcitation.org/6ali00X2L>. Accessed March 2015.

Postscapes.com. <http://postscapes.com/internet-of-things-history>. Accessed March 2015.

Rich, D., & Harris, J. (2010). *Why predictive analytics is a game-changer.* <http://www.webcitation.org/6aliFxboX>. Accessed April 2015.

Romer, P. (2015). <http://www.webcitation.org/6alilqyfs>. Accessed April 2015.

Rommety, G. IBM. <http://www.webcitation.org/6aliuTvEs>. Accessed April 2015.

Rubin, A. (2014). <http://www.webcitation.org/6aliywUq0>. Accessed April 2015.[8]

Spohrer, J. (2010). *Whole service.* Blog post 31 December 2010. <http://www.webcitation.org/6aljgQY0h>.

Srivastava, L. (2011). Back to the future. *Presentation at the European commission internet of things conference in Budapest,* May 16, 2011. <http://www.webcitation.org/6aljpF9sE>.

Turk, V. (2014). Tim Berners-Lee wants a world wide web where our data works for us. Motherboard, October 8, 2014. <http://www.webcitation.org/6aljv6hUB>. Accessed 9 April 2015.

United Nations Population Fund (UNFPA) Website. <http://www.webcitation.org/6alkSkW70>. Accessed 22.03.15.

Wall Street Journal. <http://www.webcitation.org/6alkYotRg>. Accessed 18.03.15.

---

[8] Reprint Courtesy of International Business Machines Corporation, © 2014 International Business Machines Corporation.

# CHAPTER 5

# Credit, Community, and Questions

*Science is not only a disciple of reason but, also, one of romance and passion.*

*Stephen Hawking*

## THE GROUND WORK: GIVING CREDIT

I had wanted to ask for opinions and insights from leading Service Science thinkers for this last chapter. But there are now so many of them I would have needed to write another book. And someone already had. Paul Maglio, Jim Spohrer, and Cheryl Kieliszewski published the seminal work on Service Science, *The Handbook of Service Science*, in 2010. The list of contributors reads like an all-star line-up:

Melissa A. Akaka — John Bailey — Guruduth Banavar — Rahul C. Basole — William J. Baumol — Gaurav Bhalla — Mary Jo Bitner — Jeannette Blomberg — David E. Bowen — John R. Bryson — Richard B. Chase — Henry Chesbrough — Eng K. Chew — Daniel Connors — Peter W. Daniel — Andrew Davies — Faridah Djellal — Bo Edvardsson — Shelley Evenson — Ray P. Fisk — Faïz Gallouj — Susanne Glissmann — Robert J. Glushko — Michael Gorma — Michael Gregory — Dwayne D. Gremler — Steve J. Grove — Gerhard, Gudergan — Evert Gummesson — Anders Gustafsson — Alan Hartman — James L. Heskett — Kazuyoshi Hidaka — Barbara Jones — Uday S. Karmarkar — Per Kristensson — Robert F. Lusch — Linda Macaulay — Richard Metters — Ian Miles — Aleksandra Mojsilovic — Claire Moxham — Rogelio Oliva — Lakshmish Ramaswamy — Guangjie Ren — William B. Rouse — Roland T. Rust — Scott E. Sampson — Pamela Samuelson — Jorge Sanz — W. Earl Sasser Jr — Benjamin Schneider — Carl J. Schramm — John D. Sterman — Stephen L. Vargo — Lars Witell — Valarie Zeithaml — Anatoly Zherebtsov.

Some of these authors were quoted or mentioned in this book, though it was outside our scope to include them all. So here they are, you can read their chapters in the *Handbook* and follow up on the research they have published since then. This list expands and completes the names that Jim Spohrer listed in Chapter 2.

You will notice that he does not mention his own name in any of the lists. So I would like to include this modest appraisal of Dr James ("Jim") C. Spohrer, IBM Innovation Champion and Director of IBM University Programs World Wide.

I was particularly impressed with the story of the birth of Service Science. Jim Spohrer, Paul Maglio, and others are considered to be the main founders of this discipline. It was Henry Chesbrough who told Jim to make this a discipline in the same way that IBM had begun computer science in the 1950s, and it was Spohrer and Chesbrough who wrote the *Service Science Research Manifesto* (2006). Chesbrough is best known as the father of open innovation and his book *Open Services Innovation* (2011) looks at innovation trends in services in advanced economies.

Jim Spohrer appears in every major turn that this new discipline has taken. His current research priorities include applying Service Science to create smarter (less waste and more capabilities) universities and cities, also known as tightly coupled holistic service systems that provide "whole service" to the people within them. He has more than 90 publications, including the book *The Handbook of Service Science* with co-editors Maglio and Kieliszewski. He has been awarded six patents, and is a Fellow of the Service Research and Innovation Institute (SRII). He has given numerous keynote and plenary speeches, and guest university course lectures on the founding and vision for the future of the emerging field of Service Science. He participates in numerous government, university, and other advisory roles and boards.

During the 1990s while at Apple Computer, he was awarded Apple's Distinguished Engineer Scientist and Technology title for his work on next-generation learning platforms.

Jim seems to be on all fronts. Everywhere I looked, he was there—presenting, speaking, writing—available and generous with his knowledge and expertise. He approaches from many different perspectives—philosophy, science, mathematics, engineering, the social sciences, and more—he does walk the transdisciplinary talk. He describes himself in one word: curious.

## THE COMMUNITY
### International Society of Service Innovation Professionals

A new professional association, the International Society of Service Innovation Professionals (ISSIP), fortuitously pronounced iZip, serves as an "umbrella organization interconnecting other professional societies and research centres to promote service innovation globally." This is the meeting point for Service Science and all things service. It was cofounded by IBM, Cisco, Hewlett-Packard, and several universities. Its mission is "to promote Service Innovation for our interconnected world," and "to help institutions and individuals to grow and be successful in our global service economy."

A visit to ISSIP (http://www.webcitation.org/6accAxXna) is a must if you want to get into the activities, findings, people, and knowledge that are happening today. This is a professional association that is designed on T-shaped principles, breaking away from the usual i-shaped design of specialized associations. ISSIP encourages and helps members to be part of a global network of T-shaped people in a powerful way. It is open to students, academics, business, industry, and anyone interested in service innovation, and as acts as a community of practice using social media. Their Twitter account is alive with daily tweets about interesting topics. Membership is free. Ambassadors are named from one discipline to a completely different discipline in order to promote ideas, competence, and teamwork across the board.

When you click the ISSIP Learning Center menu and scroll down to Datasets, you will find an amazing collection of open datasets on service from across the Web done by Jim Spohrer, Haluk Demirkan, and Dianne Fodell. As of April 2014, there were over 80 datasets listed, with its link and a brief description. This list truly reflects the multi-, inter-, and transdisciplinary outlook of service innovation. A few examples of the wealth of information you can access here include open datasets from Alpha Data, Carnegie Mellon University, Comprehensive Knowledge Archive Network (CKAN), Crunch Base, Databib, European Commission Eurostat, Freebase, Government of Canada Open Data Pilot, IBM Many Eyes, Infochimps, Learnlab Science of Learning Centre, MusicBrainz, Open Genomes Data, Librarything, United Nations Data Set, US National Library of Medicine, and World Bank.

An enjoyable way to learn more about Service Science can be found in ISSIP's Speakers Series with Jim Spohrer and Yassi Moghaddam, Executive Director of ISSIP.

If you want a quick overview—only 2 to 4 minutes for each video—Jim answers Yassi's questions on the evolution of service research at IBM, iTrends and future jobs, services dominant work, innovation, and advice to professionals.

## Special Interest Groups

Many professional associations are adding Service Science special interest groups (SIGS), conferences, and journals related to Service Science. Some examples include the Services SIG (SERVSIG) of the American Marketing Association; the Institute for Operations Research and the Management Sciences (INFORMS), which has a section on Service Science; the Production and Operation Management Society (POMS) College of Service Operations, which has held 12 International Research Symposiums on Service Excellence in Management; the IT Service Management Forum (itSMF), an internationally recognized forum for IT service management professionals worldwide; and the Technology Services Industry Association (TSIA), which provides benchmarking and research, peer networking, and learning opportunities.

## California Center for Service Science

Led by the School of Engineering at the University of California, Merced, and the Rady School of Management at University of California, San Diego, the University of California has established the California Center for Service Science, a virtual, cross-campus organization aimed at advancing the frontier of service research and education.

The following is taken from their website (http://ccss.ucmerced.edu):

> *Although the service sector in California accounts for more than 80% of the jobs and more than 80% of the GDP, the service sector is understudied and the service workforce is undereducated in the state. Several University of California campuses, including Berkeley, Los Angeles, San Diego, Davis, and Merced, offer Service-Science related courses, but there is currently no organized center for education and research on service at UC or in California more broadly. By creating a cross-campus center aligned with industry and government needs in the broad areas of knowledge-based and innovative service systems, the Center will advance the frontier of Service Science research and leadership in this emerging area. The Center will also educate the workforce to fit California's economic needs, establishing an organization that will be self-sustaining through government and industry partnerships, and powering an engine of skill, innovation, and job growth for the state and the nation.*

An interview with Paul Maglio concerning the CCSS can be found on the ISSIP website, http://www.webcitation.org/6accLpcGz.

## Centers and Networks

Besides the California Center for Service Science, university-affiliated service centers and academic-oriented networks are being established around the world; for example, the Centre for Service Management at Loughborough University in the United Kingdom. Collaborative organizations have also been developed, such as the Service Research and Innovation Institute (SRII; www.thesrii.org), a global, nonprofit organization that has members from industry, academia, research institutes, and government organizations. SRII's mission is to "Drive research and innovation for IT enabled services for a better world." SRII is led by senior leaders from major IT companies including Google, Amazon, Apple, Facebook, Intel, Citrix, Microsoft, IBM, HP, Infosys, TCS, eBay/PayPal, Accenture, among others, in close partnership with academia, research institutes, as well as government organizations from around the world.

## Swiss Institute of Service Science

The Swiss Institute of Service Science (SISS), www.servicescience.ch is a unique think tank that was established by five Swiss research institutes that have worked successfully in different fields of the service economy, each having a history of interdisciplinary research. Members of the association are public or private organizations active in the field of Service Science. Currently, all members of SISS are research institutes from different Swiss universities. Companies or public entities may choose to become "strategic partners" of SISS, and individual memberships are also granted to people who are active in this field.

The goal of SISS is to create service innovation by addressing a specific innovative idea with a company that will lead to a new service offer. Company experts and academic specialists work hand in hand to create practical solutions for that environment.

In most cases several experts from different disciplines and a specific project team that is composed of company employees and researchers are working together.

## Karlsruhe Service Research Institute

Faculty members at Karlsruhe Institute of Technology (KIT) created the Karlsruhe Service Research Institute (KSRI) in 2008 to conduct research and offer specialized Service Science modules for undergraduate and graduate students within the school's industrial engineering, information management, and technical economics degree programs. The goal is to create "T-shaped" people who have deep knowledge in one or two areas of study, and some level of expertise and communications skills in related areas.

## SOME QUESTIONS

I interviewed Jim Spohrer for this book, thinking it would make a good final chapter. His answers to my questions were so knowledgeable and thorough we decided to divide up the interview and include some of his comments in the chapters that spoke of those issues. However there were four questions that I saved for the end, and here they are.

## Service Science in iSchools

Of course I had to ask Jim Spohrer his opinion on a home for Service Science. The question I asked him was: Does a faculty, department, or school exist that could encompass the interdisciplinary scope of Service Science? For example, could Service Science find a proper "home" in iSchools?

And his answer:

> *Irene Ing at Warwick said it best—Service Science is a transdiscipline—as such the parts are changed (Service Science can take root in any discipline home from marketing to operations to computer science) and as such the whole is changed (Service Science can start top down, as a new discipline, school, or area of study)…*
> **So yes, it can take root in the iSchool or anywhere else…**
> *It can also start as a major new school or center….*

## Jobs of the Future

The question: What would you recommend to young people contemplating their choice of study today? What are going to be the jobs of the future?

*I would recommend students stick to the classic disciplines—that will make finding a job easier—but make sure they seek out and take courses related to Service Science, smarter planet, smarter cities, cloud computing, analytics, and get experience in an emerging market nation or a developed nation (whichever is different from where they were raised)... I wrote a piece (small opinion piece on advice to students) that appeared in the Chronicle of Higher Education...*

*That said, some students—a few who may be the future Newton, Maxwell, or Einstein of Service Science should take as many disciplines as they can, get as much real world experience as they can—meet Steve Vargo, Bob Lusch, Irene Ing, Bob Glushko, Evert Gummeson, Christian Gronross, Scott Sampson, Roland Rust, Mary Jo Bitner, Jim Tien, Daniel Berg, and I could add another 50 names... and then try to make the breakthrough linking Ricardo's Law of Comparative Advantage to Evolution the formation of hierarchical complex systems and various other ingredients that we know must be integrated to achieve a truly deep and comprehensive science of service systems and value-cocreation...*

*I would also recommend that students try to be T-shaped with depth and breadth (see http://www.webcitation.org/6accVbgVa). I would recommend if they want technical depth to consider CCAMSS areas—Cognitive Cloud Analytics Mobile Social Secure—many job opportunities for the future.*

*Also, I would encourage them to learn how to build cognitive assistants for all occupations in smart service systems (http://www.webcitation.org/6accbGOiN and http://www.webcitation.org/6accgHuVV).*

## Smart Universities

The question: You speak of "smart universities" that contribute to smart cities. Is there a description or a definition of smart universities, better yet, examples that would help us understand what they should be?

The reply:

*See this: http://www.webcitation.org/6acclm0H0*
*And this: http://www.webcitation.org/6accqS6rs*
*And this: http://www.webcitation.org/6acd5V07k*
*I would say you can recognize smart universities today in several ways:*
  *(1) They are one of the top five employers in their city or state...*
  *(2) They have a medical school and hospital as part of the university...*
  *(3) They have a top-ranked incubator and new venture launch program... http://www.webcitation.org/6acdH4IAo*
  *(4) They have as many or more on-line students as students on-campus http://www.webcitation.org/6acdO8q2f*
  *(5) They have strong connections linking developed and emerging markets http://www.webcitation.org/6acdpfzx8*
  *(6) They are a living lab that connects the university and the regions with relevant innovation.*

*See Richard Florida's "Who's Your City" (http://www.webcitation.org/ 6acg581wh) and this YouTube: http://www.webcitation.org/6acgEddOr.*

## 2007 White Paper Recommendations

The question: The White Paper that resulted from the Cambridge Service Science, Management and Engineering Symposium that IBM and the University of Cambridge Institute for Manufacturing held in 2007 put forth recommendations for the development of this science. It stressed collaboration across academic disciplines and a doubling of investment in service education and research by government and business.

Have you seen the application of these recommendations in the 8-year interval since the symposium?

The reply:

*Absolutely, we reported on this in the update of that article in the book* Handbook of Service Science—*Korea, Taiwan, Singapore, Finland, and even the United States have made great progress...*

*Here is a fun historical document that most people do not know about— Ginni Rometty is our new CEO at IBM...*

*http://www.ibm.com/ibm/governmentalprograms/pdf/ Issue_Paper_Services_Science_v.1.0.pdf Outside IBM—this has become one of the most viewed and cited papers in the Journal of Service Research:*

*http://www.webcitation.org/6acgfJbrU*

*http://www.webcitation.org/6acgnhC93*

*Most recently NSF (National Science Foundation in the US) is funding more work in the area of "smart service systems" to build innovation capacity for smart service systems between academics, industry, and government.*

*See also: http://www.webcitation.org/6acgsjZoN.*

*There is a service-related conference somewhere in the world every week...*

*There are over two dozen professional associations with Service Science related Special Interest Groups (SIGS); see http://www.webcitation.org/ 6ach0nadp.*

It would appear that Service Science is well anchored and that its exponential growth will surely continue.

Our journey to learn about Service Science has come full circle. First of all, you now know it exists, and when someone asks you "what's Service Science" you will have an idea as to how to answer. Services and service systems that we take for granted merit being looked at in a different way. Services need attention and study as much as manufacturing did in the industrial era, and this is for the common good. Information professionals especially need to know, research, and communicate the elements of Service Science in their work. The fascinating story of how the next technology trends interplay with Service Science to make a smarter planet is of tremendous social value and meaning. The future is an exciting one, and so *interesting*. May you contribute to, participate in, and enjoy *your* part in this journey. "Come on in, the water is fine!"

## REFERENCES

Chesbrough, H. (2011). *Open services innovation* San Francisco, CA: Jossey-Bass.
Chesbrough, H., & Spohrer, J. (2006). A research manifesto for services science. *Communications of the ACM, 49*(7), 35—40.
Hobohm, H.C. (2015). *Service science as a transdisciplinary model for information science.* <http://www.webcitation.org/6achBIe2u> Accessed May 2015.
Maglio, P., & Kieliszewski, C. (Eds.), (2015). *Handbook of service business: Management, marketing, innovation and internationalization* Cheltenham: Edward Elgar Publishing.
Maglio, P., Spohrer, J., & Kieliszewski, C. (2010). *The handbook of service science* New York, NY: Springer.

# EPILOGUE

How do we end a book on a topic that just keeps growing faster and faster? Every time I looked around, there was another study, article, book, or opinion that merited attention and inclusion. You must have a cut-off point somewhere, and this is it. It is reassuring however to know that Service Science is thriving in and through so many disciplines.

Let's wrap up our time together with some final thoughts.

The concept of the knowledge burden, I believe, is part of the responsibility of the information professional in all disciplines and systems. What is the knowledge burden? In 1676, Isaac Newton wrote to Robert Hooke, "*If I have seen further it is by standing on the shoulders of giants.*" Jones (2005) suggests that "*if one is to stand on the shoulders of giants, one must first climb up their backs, and the greater the body of knowledge, the harder this climb becomes.*"

Although it is easy to transfer our physical goods to the next generation, it is not as easy to transfer our knowledge. The total stock of knowledge today is far greater than in Newton's time. The knowledge burden of a society stems from the necessity to transmit the knowledge required to maintain all systems and to continue to innovate in order to ensure the quality of life for their generation as well as the future generations.

To return to the quotation in Chapter 1, "*From Lascaux to YouTube the story is the same: I was here, and I have a story to tell*" (Rubin, 2010). How will access to this precious knowledge be given, in all fields, in all times? I had the immense pleasure to go to Google's headquarters in Mountain View a few years ago to present a project, the Global Health Library, from the World Health Organization. What an amazing experience for an information geek—or anyone for that matter. The relevant point here is that when I asked who the main hires were, I was told that the majority were engineers and librarians. What a winning combination this is! There is so much to learn in stepping out of our silos. The engineers seemed to enjoy this as well.

The website of an international organization I know well only got going in those early days when the responsible team was made up of the head of IT, the head of the Library, and the head of Public Information. The energetics that ensued produced an award-winning website long before any other agency even had one.

These two examples are given to encourage a transdisciplinary mindset because together we can figure it all out. Information professionals are highly "marriageable" and come with a magnificent dowry.

## WE'VE ONLY JUST BEGUN

It is good to watch the waves that flow over our time and our lives. Some of us know these waves are coming, but most of us are living our lives, busy being busy. And that is OK. Every once in a while though, as we come up for air, as we read something that hits us both intellectually and in our solar plexus, as someone makes a comment that imprints itself on our thought patterns, as our children show us how their generation is moving ahead at great speed, we notice that something has changed. There has been a shift. The shift includes big data, analytics, cloud, mobile, social media, security, and cognitive computing. We are in the cognitive era. And the shift in consciousness—quiet, enormous—envelopes the whole.

As information specialists, we lived the coming of computer systems and the digital age. We saw the first generation of computers that were computational—they mainly counted. Then we saw computers that were programmed—the programs that went in, and the results that came out. Now we are in the era of cognitive computing, and we will be seeing the mind-boggling results of computers that we are teaching to think.

The repercussions of the research in this young Service Science are far reaching. Although the concept of Service Science is intellectually stimulating, it is rewarding on other levels as well. The enthusiasm of the ideas put forth by the movers and shakers of Service Science is contagious, and flows into ways of bettering society and solving problems that this planet is facing. Meaning is important to our work; it is important to all human beings having achieved a level of survival and safety. Making a difference is a cherished value in our society.

We have travelled a bit of the road together. We began by looking at service and services, pointing out all that we have and enjoy that we have not necessarily called services. Then we investigated service systems, which make up the basic building blocks of Service Science. The amazing story of how Service Science began took us on a journey as big as IBM and the IBM'ers that got excited about it, and as small as the systems that are us as individuals and families. And since this is a book for information professionals, we had a whole chapter on the parallels, synergies, and logical affiliations between Service Science and the information sciences. Then a very nice happening—that a smarter planet was coming into being, that this was already happening, and the smarter cities, smarter schools, smarter everything were part of the shift. The last chapter, in ending our story, gives credit, appreciation, and a few pointers to what else is coming.

We have travelled from the microcosm of the element called service and its place in systems, to the macrocosm of a science of service benefitting society. There is still much to discover as Service Science continues. You have a good general introduction in this book, and many avenues from which to further explore this phenomenon.

My wish for you, in the spirit of the quotation from Stephen Hawking at the beginning of Chapter 5, is that your story with Service Science be stimulating to your intellectual curiosity yet with a little mix of the passion and romance that makes the world go round.

**Yvonne de Grandbois**
Céligny, Switzerland
May 2015

## REFERENCES

Jones B.F. (2005). The burden of knowledge and the 'death of the renaissance man': is innovation getting harder? NBER Working Paper, No. 11360. May.

Rubin, R. (2010). *Foundations of library and information science* (3rd ed.) New York, NY: Neal-Schuman Publishers.

# INDEX

## A

Academic home for Service Science, 62
AGORA (Access to Global Online Research in Agriculture), 24
Agricultural revolution, 27
Amazon, 20, 33, 55–56, 85
Analytics, 76–77, 84–85
  descriptive, 84
  predictive, 85
  prescriptive, 85
ARDI (Access to Research for Development and Innovation), 24
ATM. *See* Automated teller machine (ATM)
Automated teller machine (ATM), 12

## B

Back office, 17
"Back to the Future", 78
Benefits of Service Science, 43–44
Berners-Lee, Tim, 82–83
Big data, 81–84
*Big Data at Work*, 82
Blue Trunk Libraries, 23
Boeing Aeronautics, 8
Business, servitization of, 30–31
*Business Insider*, 81
Business service, 2

## C

California Center for Service Science, 102–103
Carnegie public libraries, 22–23
Center for Services Leadership (CSL), 69
Centers and networks, 103
CERN, 83–84
Charter Cities Initiative, 92
Chesbrough, Henry, 100
Circular economy, 87
Cisco Systems, 58
Claas tractor, 78
Client-based relationship, 10
Cloud computing, 13, 85–86
  service categories of, 86
Cognitive computing, 86

Community
  California Center for Service Science, 102–103
  centers and networks, 103
  International Society of Service Innovation Professionals (ISSIP), 101–102
  Karlsruhe Service Research Institute (KSRI), 104
  special interest groups, 102
  Swiss Institute of Service Science (SISS), 103
Computer science, 37–38, 42, 63
Computer Science and Artificial Intelligence Laboratory (CSAIL), 83
Computer systems design engineering, 6
Contrarians, 44
CSAIL. *See* Computer Science and Artificial Intelligence Laboratory (CSAIL)
CSL. *See* Center for Services Leadership (CSL)
Customer contact, 10
Customer-led economy, 11

## D

Data/information/knowledge/wisdom (DIKW) triangle, 76–77
Decision-making abilities, 86
Delphi technique, 61
Deutsche Telekom and Canyon Bicycles, 78
Dornbracht's digitally controlled bathroom, 78
Durkopp Adler sewing machine, 78

## E

Economic crisis (1973), 29
Economic importance of services, 29–30
Economic sectors, types of, 28–29
Economy and Service Science, 48
Educational services, 1
Engagement, 86
Ethnomethodology, 19–20

## F

The Food and Agriculture Organization (FAO), 24
*Foreign Affairs*, 80–81
Freedom economy, 57
Front office, 17
FAO. *See* The Food and Agriculture Organization (FAO)

## G

GE, 8
Geneva School of Business Administration, Switzerland, 67
God particle, 83–84
Goods and services, differentiation between, 7
Google, 33, 55–56, 85
Goul, Michael, 57
Greenberg, Sherri, 91

## H

*The Handbook of Service Science*, 100
Healthcare and medical service, 1
HINARI Access to Research in Health, 24
History of Service Science, 27, 40–41
  agricultural, industrial, and post-industrial economies, 27–28
  basic components, 41–43
  beneficiaries, 43–44
  economic importance of services, 29–30
  economic sectors, types of, 28–29
  getting started, 39
    CONNECT section, 39
    LEARN section, 39
    TEACH section, 39
  IBM story, 37–39
  knowledge economy, 27
  reasons for shift, 31–33
  satisfaction, 44–45
  service and knowledge, economy of, 34–37
  service sector, rise of, 31
  servitization of business, 30–31
  tandem with shift, 33–34
Holistic service systems, 17
*Horizon Report*, 81
Hospitality and leisure services, 2
Hybrid cloud, 85

## I

IBM, 8, 36–39, 86–88
ICT. *See* Information and communication technology (ICT)
IDEO design firm, 60
IFTF. *See* Institute for the Future (IFTF)
Industrial models, 68
Industrial phase, 27–28
Information, communications, and technology, 1
Information and communication technology (ICT), 52–53
Information Networks for Knowledge Department, 23
Information professionals and service, 47–48, 51–52
Information work, service systems in, 21
INFORMS. *See* Institute for Operations Research and the Management Sciences (INFORMS)
Institute for Operations Research and the Management Sciences (INFORMS), 102
Institute for the Future (IFTF), 61
Instrumentation, 95
Integrator Global, 91
Intelligence, 95
Interconnectedness, 95
International information sector, 23–24
International Society of Service Innovation Professionals (ISSIP), 101–102
Internet, 5, 13, 21, 78, 85
Internet of Things (IoT), 75–78
iSchools/Information schools, 62–64
  proposal, 64–66
  Service Science in, 104
  teaching at, 70–71
ISSIP. *See* International Society of Service Innovation Professionals (ISSIP)
IT Service Management Forum (itSMF), 102

## J

Jobs of the future, 104–105

## K

Karlsruhe Service Research Institute (KSRI), 104
Knowledge brokers, 49–50
Knowledge economy, 27, 34–37
   and life-long learning, 22–23
Knowledge sharing, necessity for, 9–10
Knowledge workers, 34–35, 44
   new profile for, 59–61
Knowledge-based services, 35
KSRI. *See* Karlsruhe Service Research Institute (KSRI)
Kucharvy, Tom, 89

## L

Large Hadron Collider (LHC), 83–84
Leisure and recreational services, 2
LHC. *See* Large Hadron Collider (LHC)
Librarianship, 19, 63
Library 2.0 and long tail, 20–21
Library 3.0, 22
Long tail, 20–21
   application to information work, 21

## M

Maglio, Paul, 55, 68, 99–100, 103
Mayo Clinic, 55–56
McLuhan, Marshall, 80

## N

Netflix, 20, 55–56
North American Industry Classification System (NAICS code), 5

## O

OARE (Online Access to Research in the Environment), 24
*Open Services Innovation*, 100
Organizational models, 8–9

## P

PayPal, 55–56
PetSmart, p225
Piggly-Wiggly, 12
Post-industrial economy, 28

Private cloud services, 85
Production and Operation Management Society (POMS) College of Service Operations, 102
"Production" of services, 8–9
Productive/unproductive labor, 7
Product-service continuum, 7–8
Professional association, 101–102, 106
Professional services, 2
Public cloud providers, 85

## R

Republic Services, Inc., 57
Research4Life, 24
Research and development services, 30
Research opportunities, 49–50
Research priorities, in services, 50–58
   creating and maintaining service culture, 53–54
   effectively branding and selling services, 55–56
   enhancing the service experience through co-creation, 56
   fostering service infusion and growth, 51–52
   improving well-being through transformative service, 52–53
   leveraging technology to advance service, 57
   service design, enhancing, 54–55
   service innovation, stimulating, 54
   service networks and value chains, optimizing, 55
   value of service, measuring and optimizing, 57
Robochop, 78

## S

Self-service, 12–13
Self-service technologies (SSTs), 12–13
Service(s), 1–2
   applying long tail to information work, 21
   attributes, 3
   business, 2
   classifying, 4
      marketing and economics, 4–5

Service(s) (*Continued*)
  contact factor, 10
  definition, 2–3
  economic importance of, 29–30
  economy of, 34–37
  education, 1
  food, 2
  healthcare and medical, 1
  hospitality and leisure, 2
  IHIP paradigm, 3–4
  inseparability, 3–4
  intangible, 3
  international information sector, 23–24
  knowledge economy and life-long learning, 22–23
  Library 2.0 and long tail, 20–21
  Library 3.0, 22
  organizational models, 8–9
  perishable, 4
  personalization of, 3
  Piggly-Wiggly, 12
  products and, 7
  product-service continuum, 7–8
  professional, 2
  public, 1
  Research4Life, 24
  retail and wholesale, 2
  risk factors, 9–10
  self-service, 12
  self-service technologies (SSTs), 12–13
  service system. *See* Service system
  services-dominant view, 10–11
  Standard Industrial Classification (SIC), 5–6
  super service, 13
  sustainability and, 14
  trade of goods and services, 6
  typologies of, 6
Service Lab, 67
Service Research and Innovation Institute (SRII), 100, 103
Service Science
  Internet of Things (IoT), 77–78
    practical applications of, 79–80
  for smarter planet, 75–77
  and social value, 93–94

Service Science, Management, and Engineering (SSME), 40
  degree programs, 66
Service Science, Management, Engineering, and Design (SSME + D), 40
Service Science and information sector, synergies between, 47
  academic home for Service Science, 62
  economy and Service Science, 48
  information professionals and service, 47–48
  iSchools/Information schools, 62–64
    proposal, 64–66
    teaching at, 70–71
  knowledge worker, new profile for, 59–61
  libraries, studying, 72–73
  new vistas of energy, 49
  outside opinion, 72
  partnerships, 50
  research opportunities, 49–50
  research priorities in services, 50–58
    creating and maintaining service culture, 53–54
    effectively branding and selling services, 55–56
    enhancing the service experience through co-creation, 56
    fostering service infusion and growth, 51–52
    improving well-being through transformative service, 52–53
    leveraging technology to advance service, 57
    service design, enhancing, 54–55
    service innovation, stimulating, 54
    service networks and value chains, optimizing, 55
    value of service, measuring and optimizing, 57
  Service Lab, 67
  Service Science explosion, 47
  Service Science in iSchools, 104
  *Service Science Research Manifesto*, 100
  Service sector, rise of, 13, 31

Service system, 14–15, 40–41, 65–66
　and functions, 15–17
　growth of, 17–18
　holistic, 17
　in information work, 18–20
Services SIG (SERVSIG), 102
Servitization of business, 30–31
Servitization of products, 7–8
SERVSIG. *See* Services SIG (SERVSIG)
SIC. *See* Standard Industrial Classification (SIC)
SIGS. *See* Special interest groups (SIGS)
Singapore Management University, 70–71
SISS. *See* Swiss Institute of Service Science (SISS)
Smart universities, 105–106
Smarter Cities, 89–92
Smarter Planet Initiative, 87–89
Social media, 11
Social value, 93–94
Special interest groups (SIGs), 102
Spohrer, Jim, 99–101, 104
SRII. *See* Service Research and Innovation Institute (SRII)
SSME. *See* Service Science, Management, and Engineering (SSME)
SSME + D. *See* Service Science, Management, Engineering, and Design (SSME + D)
SSTs. *See* Self-service technologies (SSTs)
Standard Industrial Classification (SIC), 5–6
Starbucks, 55–56
Super service, 13
Sustainability, 18
　and services, 14
Swiss Institute of Service Science (SISS), 103

**T**
TANK, Australian brand agency, 60
Taylor model, 8–9
Technology Services Industry Association (TSIA), 102
Tech target, 86
Tesla, Nikola, 80
Trade of goods and services, 6

Transformative service research (TSR), 52–53, 93
Transportation systems, 1
T-shaped professionals, 60–61
TSIA. *See* Technology Services Industry Association (TSIA)
TSR. *See* Transformative service research (TSR)
Turing, Alan, 80

**U**
UNEP. *See* United Nations Environmental Programme (UNEP)
Unified Service Theory (UST) paradigm, 4
United Nations Environmental Programme (UNEP), 24
University of Boras, Sweden, 62
University of California Berkeley, 64–65, 70
University of Toronto, 64–65, 70–71
*Using Innovation and Technology to Improve City Services*, 91

**V**
Value propositions, 15, 40

**W**
*Wall Street Journal*, 78–79
Wal-Mart, 82
Watson computer, 86
2007 White Paper recommendations, 106–107
Whole service cities, 92–93
WIPO. *See* World Intellectual Property Organization (WIPO)
WLCG. *See* Worldwide LHC Computing Grid (WLCG)
World Health Organization (WHO) Library, 23–24
World Intellectual Property Organization (WIPO), 24
Worldwide LHC Computing Grid (WLCG), 83–84
WP Carey School of Business, Arizona State University, 50–51, 69

**Y**
Yahoo, 55–56

Edwards Brothers Malloy
Thorofare, NJ USA
November 17, 2015